Editorial Project Manager
Elizabeth Morris, Ph. D.

Editor-in-Chief
Sharon Coan, M.S. Ed.

Cover Artist
Lesley Palmer

Imaging
Alfred Lau

Production Manager
Phil Garcia

Publisher
Mary D. Smith, M.S. Ed.

W9-BSG-938

1001 Best Websites for Educators

3rd Edition

Author

Timothy Hopkins

Teacher Created Resources

Teacher Created Resources, Inc.
6421 Industry Way
Westminster, CA 92683

ISBN-0-7439-3877-1

©2005 Teacher Created Resources, Inc.
Reprinted, 2005
Made in U.S.A.

www.teachercreated.com
URL updates available at our website

Table of Contents

Foreword 3
Categories 4
Art 9
Career Resources 22
Child Development 32
Classroom and Behavior Management 40
Diversity in the Classroom 49
Early Childhood. 60
Education Laws, Regulations, and Standards 65
Funding Sources 70
Geography/Environment 79
Government 90
History and Social Studies 97
Language Arts 109
Lesson Plans 118
Mathematics. 127
Multimedia. 135
Multimedia Enhanced Sites. 137
Music 139
Organizations. 148
Publications 159
Reading First 174
Research and Reference Resources. 180
Science. 191
Searching the Web. 203
Sites for Students. 208
Software. 217
Special Education 222
Teaching. 230
Technology 239
Test Practice. 249
Writing. 254

Foreword

Welcome to the latest and greatest collection of education-related websites. With more than 1,000 websites, all representing the best the Web has to offer, this book is an indispensable resource for the wired teacher.

This third edition presents three new categories. The sites found in the **Early Childhood** section can help you prepare young children for kindergarten. The No Child Left Behind Act and Reading First Initiative are attempting a whole new era in education, and the **Reading First** section contains more than 20 sites where you can learn more about implementing them in your classroom. Preparing your students for the SAT, ACT, or other standardized tests? Or looking for an easier way to create tests in your classroom? The **Test Practice** section can help you.

With all of the resources in this book, you're sure to find enough websites to make your online time more useful. And don't forget—by buying this book you're entitled to free updates. Because the Internet changes so rapidly and Web sites are often short-lived, you may find that some of the sites have moved or have disappeared altogether. If this is the case, you will find new addresses or be provided with replacement sites.

Updates can be found at the publisher's website at
http://www.teachercreated.com/
Click on URL Updates, and enter the number of this book, 3877. This will take you to an index page where you can find links to updated sites.

Categories

Art

This section contains all things about art, and the list of quality art sites just keeps getting longer and longer. To make room for all of them, we've moved the music sites to their own category.

Career Resources

The Web has made job hunting much easier, though still not painless. Prospective job applicants in the education field have many sites from which to choose. There are the massive jobs sites, like *Headhunter.net*, with hundreds of thousands of listings. There are also sites, such as *K–12jobs.com*, that cater just to educators. The sites listed here have more than a million job postings, and one might be the right job for you!

Child Development

Some education-related websites are of interest only to teachers of the very young. To make these resources easier to locate, I created the Child Development section and populated it with more than 40 sites that represent the many valuable resources you'll find on the Web.

Classroom and Behavior Management

The primary concern of new teachers is often effective classroom management practices. Usually, they are learned either by experience or with help from others. Fortunately, practicing teachers and other experts have created the sites and pages listed here in an effort to share what they have learned about managing a classroom.

Diversity

It's a big world out there and American classrooms often reflect this diversity in their student populations. The sites listed here represent some of the best websites you can find to gather information about the many cultures of the world and the diverse cultures of the students you may find in your classes.

Early Childhood

It's never too early to start learning! Give a young child a head start at succeeding in school with these sites. The activities, resources, and tips found at these sites provide a strong background for the young learner.

Education Laws

Every profession has rules to live by, and education is no exception. Whether researching the Americans with Disabilities Act or reviewing the National Standards, there's a lot of guidance and information to be found at these sites.

Funding

A little money goes a long way in the classroom. Unfortunately, that money seldom drops from the sky into your lap. Instead, you'll have to visit these quality sites to find potential funding opportunities just waiting for proposals.

Geography/Environment

Every year this category keeps getting larger, with new, great places to visit popping up on a regular basis. Whether they're from PBS, National Geographic, or someone's personal site, the resources here for teachers and students represent the best the Web has to offer.

Government

Governmental institutions were early adopters of the Internet and their sites reflect this early start. While totally new sites are rare, the existing sites continuously add new content to increase their value.

History and Social Studies

Whether you're looking for historical documents and maps, information on an event, or just ideas to use in the classroom, you're sure to find something of interest at these history sites. This section has been, and continues to be, one of the strongest and deepest educational areas on the Web.

Language Arts

This is another very strong area, with literally thousands of sites touching every aspect of the language arts. The best and the brightest are listed here, from children's literature to the ancient classics and everything between.

Lesson Plans

Teachers, it seems, love to share their lessons and ideas. This happy fact is reflected in sites such as Nova and NASA which attract teachers by offering their own lesson plans. This year's collection of lesson plan sites is the best it has ever been.

Mathematics

From basic operations to fractals, this group of sites has something to appeal to every math teacher (and student).

Multimedia

Every year more and more sites incorporate multimedia technology. To take advantage of these movies, sounds, etc., you'll need the software described in the first section of this category. The second section lists some of the best websites that are offering multimedia elements as part of their content.

Music

Whether you are looking for practice and theory, resources for educators and scholars, sheet music, or even events to plan for a high school band, you'll find it all and more at these music sites.

Organizations

This section contains a simple list of more than 100 education-related organizations, almost all with membership information and many with resources for teachers.

Publications

To stay current on education and the world at large, teachers have to read. We've provided links to local and world newspapers, popular magazines, and educational journals. Many of these sites provide their print content online for free!

Reading First

If you need to implement the Reading First Initiative or No Child Left Behind Act into your classroom or school, these sites can help you get started. Information on reading programs, phonics, and activities for children from birth to school age can be found here.

Research/Reference Sources

There may be nothing better about the Internet than how it assists those who do research. This group of sites will give you access to dictionaries, encyclopedias, and hundreds of other research and reference resources.

Science

You'll be blinded with science, too, after visiting these great sites. Science-related sites, it seems, are more apt to use eye-catching graphics and motion. You'll definitely want to share some of these places with your students.

Searching the Web

This book was written so you won't have to waste your valuable time searching the Web. Still, there will be times when you'll have to trust a search engine to tell you where something is located. This section provides some searching tips and has links to general and education-specific search engines.

Sites for Students

This section is written primarily for teachers who wish to integrate the Web into their teaching. These sites can be shared as a whole class, or you can bookmark them for students to visit during their independent times on the computer.

Software

If you're going to be on the Web, you're going to need software. But what kind of software do you need? This section explains the ins and outs of browsers, e-mail programs, chat clients, and more, and it points you to where you can download these programs for free.

Special Education

Special education sites continue to flourish. The sites listed here are organized by special education subcategories.

Teaching

Some sites eschew the content areas and focus mainly on the craft of teaching. This collection of teaching-related resources will benefit both the new and experienced teacher.

Technology

It's very appropriate to have a technology section in a book like this, and I've gathered the top sites that offer educational technology-related resources, including articles, tutorials, teaching tips and ideas.

Test Practice

Prepare your students for standardized tests or create your own tests with these sites.

Writing

Helping your students with a research paper? Looking for rules of grammar or tips for keeping your writing cliché-free? Both the experienced and the novice writer will find all sorts of valuable information at these sites.

Art

A. Pintura: Art Detective

http://www.eduweb.com/pintura

Designed for fourth-graders and up, this site uses a 40's film noir to teach art history (Raphael, Van Gogh, Picasso, etc.) and concepts (subject, portrait, Renaissance, etc.). This is just one of the many great resources provided by Educational Web Adventures:

http://eduweb.com/adventure.html

African Art Lesson Plans

http://members.aol.com/TWard64340/Africa.htm

Elementary art lesson plans on how to make masks, shields, and "kente" placemats. Also features links to ancient Africa.

All Oriland – Origami Galore

http://www.oriland.com

Oriland is a site devoted to origami, paper folding as art. Oriland provides detailed instructions on how to create origami figures (crystals, buildings, people, etc.). There's also information on 3-D origami and everything origami-related. Good teacher's section, too.

Art History Resources on the Web

http://witcombe.sbc.edu/ARTHLinks.html

From Prehistoric to the 21st Century, the art mega-site is a wonderful collection of links to art resources on the web. If the search engines fail you or you're just out for an Internet stroll for art, stop here and you'll find everything you could want.

Art History Theme Page

http://www.cln.org/themes/art_history.html

This site features links to other art resources on the web, including career information, art preservation, and more.

Art Kids Rule!

http://artkidsrule.com/

This is a very good site full of resources teachers can use to teach art and help kids get excited about expressing themselves. There are art tutorials, lesson plans and activities, many useful articles, and art arcades that feature painting online and other activities.

@rt Room

http://www.arts.ufl.edu/art/rt_room/

This site has gotten better and better as time passes. It features art sparkers (ideas for art lessons), a gallery of student work, art artifacts, a library, a list of related links, and more.

Art Safari

http://www.moma.org/momalearning/artsafari/

An adventure in looking, for children and adults presented by the Museum of Modern Art. Designed to be viewed by a child and a teacher or parent, questions guide you to make up stories on the artwork. Children can then write about what they see and submit their writing.

Art Teacher Connection

http://www.artteacherconnection.com

This site has grown into a very good collection of resources. Categories include National Standards, Assessment Tools, Teaching Resources, and many other art-related areas. The site is maintained by Bettie Lake, an art teacher from Phoenix.

Art Teacher on the Net

http://www.artmuseums.com

Art ideas for teachers, parents, scouts and kids. Includes sections on Art History, Project Lessons, Parent Ideas, Art Projects for Students, and a Teacher Exchange section where teachers share their ideas.

ArtLex

http://www.artlex.com

A comprehensive visual arts dictionary of over 2,800 art terms, many complete with pronunciation guides and illustrations. For example, a click on "Baroque" will result in a definition, a pronunciation, 15 illustrations, and links to many more.

Arts/Crafts for Kids (from About.com)

http://k-6educators.about.com/cs/artsandcrafts/

Links to arts and crafts sites for kids. The site reviews are informative and give a good indication of the reviewed site's usefulness. It has to be said, though, that About.com's use of pop-up and Flash ads is detracting from their sites' usefulness. The irritation level of About.com's pages is increasing.

ArtsEdge Network

http://artsedge.kennedy-center.org/artsedge.html

From the Kennedy Center, an art site featuring daily updates on arts and education news, teaching materials with standards-based curriculum, and resources for professional development, standards, guides, FAQs and more.

ArtsEdNet

http://www.getty.edu/artsednet/

This art site from the Getty Institute for the Arts, features lesson plans and curriculum ideas, image galleries (somewhat limited), and links to other WWW art sites.

Cartoon Connections

http://www.cartoonconnections.com/

A good place for students to visit, the Cartoon Connection offers lessons, tips, and printables. There's a nice cartoon gallery, too. For teachers, the site offers downloadable handouts.

CGFA Artist Index

http://cgfa.sunsite.dk/fineart.htm

This is a very nice site that features famous painters and famous paintings. The categorization is better than most other sites—artists are listed alphabetically, of course, but also by nationality and time frame. For each artist there is a biography as well as many samples of his/her art.

Children's Creative Theater

http://tqjunior.thinkquest.org/5291/

Exploring all facets of the theater, the Children's Creative Theater is a great resource for teachers (and students) interested in the theater. The site includes information on the history of theater, related terms, dramatic games to play, and skits that students can perform.

Craftnetvillage.com Project Library

http://www.craftnetvillage.com/ProjectLibrary

If you're looking for arts and craft ideas for your students, this site offers many activities with full instructions. Learn (and then teach) how to build bird house boots, spool scarecrows, and upright insects (and a lot more).

CyberKids Home

http://www.cyberkids.com

A site designed for younger kids to publish their artwork, writing, and even music (in midi format, only), this is a very highly-awarded site, one of the first and still one of the best. The site is not just about art, though. Students will find a fun and games section and links to sites that will help with their homework.

Eyes on Art

http://www.kn.pacbell.com/wired/art2

A great site for students and teachers that explores many different aspects of art, it also has interactive lessons and tips on how to use them. Categories: Visual Glossary, Artistic Styles, 2 View 4 U, Teacher's Guide, Links, Quiz.

From Windmills to Whirligigs

http://www.smm.org/sln/vollis

Offering science and art projects connected to wind, this site has virtual characters and locations as you explore windmills and whirligigs. Very well written and entertaining. Features many wraparound pictures and videos.

Global Show-n-Tell Home Page

http://telenaut.com/gst/

Making public the work a student does can lead to unexpected rewards. This page lets children show their work to kids around the world and has lots of links to children's art works on the Web.

Incredible Art Department

http://www.princetonol.com/groups/iad/

Still one of the best art sites on the web! From art news to hundreds of lesson plans, this site is a cornucopia of art resources of the Web. It contains links to over a thousand other art sites on the Web and free software downloads (for PCs and Macs).

Inside Art

http://www.eduweb.com/insideart/

An adventure in art history, Inside Art teaches painting "from the inside out" as visitors are trapped in a vortex and can only escape by asking, and answering, the "who, what, where, when" questions.

Integrating the Arts into the Classroom

http://www.op97.k12.il.us/instruct/IArts/

This site offers very detailed lesson plans with the goal of integrating the arts into various classroom topics like space, reptiles and birds, and geography.

Investigating the Renaissance

http://www.artmuseums.harvard.edu/renaissance

Using three Renaissance paintings as examples, this site illustrates how computer-assisted imaging can shed light on the process of painting. This is more for high-school and above students.

Kids Crafts Bulletin Board

http://wwvisions.com/craftbb/kids.html

This bulletin board is for the exchange of craft-related information. Post your question or respond to another's. This board is very actively used.

Kids' Gallery

http://www.kids-space.org/gallery/gallery.html

A huge gallery of art submitted by students from the world over. Sections include fantasy, abstract, science and technology, people, animal, and scenery. They've recently added a theme space which asks for pictures by theme. You can also post your artwork as a class project. A very good site.

KinderArt

http://www.kinderart.com

KinderArt offers a large collection of art lessons in many categories for many age groups. The Teachers section features a large collection of links to art articles, sites for homeschoolers and a lot more.

KinderCrafts

http://www.enchantedlearning.com/crafts/

Lots of fun craft activities for pre-K through elementary school grades. With more than 75 different craft categories, each with many activity instructions, you're sure to find some lesson ideas.

Making Friends and Other Crafts for Kids

http://www.makingfriends.com/

If you need a craft idea for students age 2-15, this site tries to deliver. There are many different craft activities here, organized alphabetically and by age level.

Marilyn's Imagination Factory

http://www.kid-at-art.com

An excellent site devoted to recycling, the Imagination Factory includes lessons, activities, and links to other art and environmental sites on the web. Be sure to check out the section on the Trashasaurus, which would make a great project for any class.

Metropolitan Museum of Art - Education

http://www.metmuseum.org/education/

If you're going to visit the Met, or just visit its online companion, this site clues you in on the educational resources available there. Also available are games and guides for kids, information on current and past exhibits, and a very nice art timeline.

Michael C. Carlos Museum

http://www.emory.edu/CARLOS/

At this site are art collections from ancient Egypt, the ancient Near East, the Sub-Sahara, and an impressive collection of art from the ancient Americas. Other Categories: History of the Museum, Classical Art, Works of Art on Paper

Monster Exchange Project

http://www.monsterexchange.org

In an excellent merging of art and writing, the Monster Exchange Project has created a wonderful website. A student draws a monster and then writes a description. Another student at a different school reads the written description and then draws the monster. The two drawings are then compared. The site also includes lesson plans and instructions on how to sign up for the program. Students from around the world participate in this site.

Mother of All Art History Links Pages

http://www.umich.edu/~hartspc/histart/mother

If you're looking for art history websites, this is a good place to start. The Mother of All... features links to sites in categories such as Art History Departments, Research Resources, Visual Collections, and Online Exhibits. This is of more use for the upper grades.

Musée du Louvre

http://www.paris.org./Musees/Louvre

This impressive resource contains most of the famous paintings housed in the Louvre, the museum's floor plan, and a short history of the museum.

Museum of Modern Art

http://www.moma.org

Very slick site with many online exhibitions that change often. A good resource, though it seems to be of more use to those who teach near the museum. They have recently been increasing their online offerings.

National Museum of American Art

http://www.nmaa.si.edu

From the Smithsonian, the National Museum of American Art offers a collection of online exhibits, a new feature collection each month, and a director's choice collection of museum favorites.

National Museum of Women in the Arts

http://www.nmwa.org

Very good site. Through the use of pictures, text, and videos, visitors learn about the contribution made by women to the arts, from the Renaissance to the late 20th century.

Perseus Project

http://www.perseus.tufts.edu

The Perseus Project is a digital library on the study of the ancient world, including its art and architecture. The site continues to expands its offerings with recent additions of the English Renaissance. This is a wonderful site that is probably most appropriate for high school grades.

Puppetry Homepage

http://www.sagecraft.com/puppetry

Just about everything you would want to know about puppets and puppetry is here. This site's most outstanding feature is its list of links to other related sites. Also featured are tips and suggestions provided by the site's users.

Rosetta Stone

http://www.clemusart.com/archive/pharaoh/rosetta

From the Cleveland Museum of Art, this site uses Rosetta Stone to teach students about Egypt through art. Students can read about Egypt, get instructions on how to build a pharaoh, and color hieroglyphics.

Scribbles

http://www.scribbleskidsart.com/

Scribbles is a great site to visit. Students can submit their artwork to the site, learn about famous artists, and even win prizes by answering a quiz or solving the Mystery Art. The site also hosts games and an online coloring book.

Smithsonian Institution

http://www.si.edu

Features links to What's New (exhibits), Perspectives, Activities, and Resources, which all provide information on a variety of subjects. Lots of graphics, sounds, and video.

Teacher's Guide for the Professional Cartoonist

http://cagle.slate.msn.com/teacher/

With helpful hints and lesson plans on how to use the Professional Cartoonists Index Website http://www.cagle.com/ in the classroom, this is a very interesting use of online information for the classroom.

Theatre on a Shoestring

http://www.geocities.com/Broadway/Balcony/6594

Thinking about putting on a play? Get advice from someone who has been there. This site offers a lot of information on high school productions of popular plays. Includes articles, a glossary, and a good forum.

Timeline of Art History

http://www.metmuseum.org/toah/

This is a beautiful presentation of art history presented by the Metropolitan Museum of Art. The interactive timeline expands with each click, providing information on the major art trends of the time.

Vincent van Gogh Information Gallery

http://www.vangoghgallery.com

From "Starry Night" to 37 different self-portraits ("Self-Portrait with Gray Felt Hat," "Self-Portrait with Straw Hat," "Self- Portrait"…you get the idea). Excellent site that has to be the best van Gogh resource on the web.

Virtual Curriculum: Elementary Art Education

http://www.dhc.net/~artgeek/

Many lesson plans and activities designed for elementary school students. Categories include The Americas, Europe, Africa, Asia, Australia, and Prehistory.

Web Museum

http://sunsite.unc.edu/wm

A first stop for anyone looking for museum-quality art on the Web, this site features rotating exhibits from the likes of Cezanne, da Vinci, and Michaelangelo. The Famous Paintings section contains thousands of examples of the most well-known Western and Japanese art, from Gothic to Pop and everything in between.

World Wide Web Virtual Library- Museums

http://www.icom.org/vlmp

A staggering list of museums on the web. Features over 600 museums in the United States alone! Also covers many other countries. This list is updated frequently and usually has reliable links. Not very well organized, though.

Career Resources

50 States' K-12 Employment Opportunities

http://www.uky.edu/Education/TEP/usajobs.html

This site can save you from having to do a lot of searching. The University of Kentucky's College of Education post links here to the K-12 job opportunities in other states. The link usually points to the centralized job announcement section of the state (if available).

Academic Employment Network

http://www.academploy.com/

While offering a listing of jobs that is not nearly as large as some of the other sites in this section, AEN is another useful resource to use in your career search. In addition to the job postings, there are professional development resources and relocation services.

Academic Position Network

http://www.apnjobs.com/

One of the oldest job sites on the Internet, APN lists job postings primarily in higher education positions. Their search engine is easy to use and the service is free to job seekers (there is a charge to post a position).

American Association of School Administrators Job Bulletin

http://www.aasa.org/apps/jobs

Primarily for school administrators, this site from AASA lists jobs throughout the country. You can search by position, location, salary, and other criteria. If you are a member, you can also receive promising job notifications via e-mail.

America's Career Infonet

http://www.acinet.org

This site offers a lot to the job seeker. The Career Exploration section alone features more than 200 career videos. State Profiles give demographic information on every state to help you gauge the job market. Another great resource is the Employability Checkup, which gives you career information based on your level of experience and geographical location. The Infonet has evolved into one of the best career resources on the web!

America's Job Bank

http://www.ajb.dni.us/

Unemployment may be up but there are just under 1 million unfilled positions in the Job Bank's database. America's Job Bank is a product of the U.S. Department of Labor and state-operated employment services. You can search for a job by occupation and by location. The site also offers many other employment resources that make it a very worthwhile visit.

Career Builder

http://www.careerbuilder.com

One of the more efficient job sites on the web, Career Builder returns search results that seem to be more applicable than the results of some other sites. The Career Advice section is particularly useful, containing articles on choosing a career, advertising yourself, interviewing, education, and more.

careerjournal from the Wall Street Journal

http://careers.wsj.com/

This site, while also being much more entertaining than the newspaper it stems from, offers more than 1,000 articles on career search, salaries, succeeding at work, and a lot more. Of particular interest is the salary calculator, which shows you average salaries on many different jobs.

CareerCity

http://www.careercity.com

Another mega job search engine offering listings from companies throughout the U.S. and Canada. What sets this site apart from the others is their Career Planning section, offering self-assessments, career management articles, and more.

CareerLab

http://www.careerlab.com/letters

Having trouble writing that cover letter? Try this site, featuring more than 200 sample cover letters for all types of positions. There are also articles on how to submit a counteroffer, how to follow-up on an interview, and many more.

CareerPath.com

http://www.careerpath.com

Tired of looking through the newspaper for a job? Try CareerPath.com. Their listings come from more than 90 of the nation's leading newspapers. You can also post your resume online for employers to view.

CEC Career Connections

http://www.cec.sped.org/cc/cc.htm

From the Council for Exceptional Children, job postings primarily for individuals in the special education field. There is also a place to post your resume, and you can view job searching tips, too.

Chronicle of Higher Education Career Network

http://thisweek.chronicle.com/jobs/

The first place to look for a position in higher education, the Chronicle usually lists more than 500 jobs a week. Subscribers get first shot at the listings, but non-subscribers can see the listings that were posted the previous week. You can also get a weekly list of jobs in your area of interest e-mailed to you.

Deaf Education Employment Opportunities

http://www.deafed.net

In addition to listing many job opportunities for professional positions within Deaf Education, there is also a section where job seekers can post their resume and describe the type of position they are looking for.

Edu Tech

http://www.edutech-1.com

EduTech is an online collection of educational employment listings for California K-12 and Community College administrative, teaching, and classified positions. Search by job title, category, or location.

Education Jobs

http://www.educationjobs.com/

This is not a free site (current charges are about $20.00 for a lifetime membership). In addition to offering many job listings, they promise a list of every school district (with contact numbers and links to websites), links to state jobs postings pages, resume building tools, and more.

Education Week Job Listings

http://www.edweek.org/jobs

The job listings here, while not nearly as numerous as those offered in the big site, are just for teachers and others looking for a position as an administrator, principal, teacher, superintendent, or for a job in higher education.

Education World Education Employment Center

http://www.education-world.com/jobs/

The Education World search engine site also has a very good career resources section that allows you to search for jobs, post your resume, check out state certification requirements, and more.

Educational/Instructional Technology Positions

http://www.aace.org/jobboard

A list of positions in the educational/instructional technology field provided by the Association for the Advancement of Computers in Education.

Educational Placement Service

http://www.educatorjobs.com/

EPS is a job placement agency that charges a fee once you have been placed in a position (probably a percentage of your income for a certain period of time— standard for most employment agencies). The site appears to have fewer listings than many other job sites in this section.

ELT Job Centre

http://www.jobs.edufind.com

If you're looking to teach English in another country, this site should be your first stop. Position listings are primarily for Asian countries, all with contact information.

Flipdog.com

http://www.flipdog.com/

Flipdog is a different type of meta-job search engine. Instead of relying on employer-submitted jobs to fill its database, Flipdog catalogs the employment section of companies' websites. Search by location, type of job, and company/school.

Higher Ed Jobs

http://www.higheredjobs.com

With more than 4,000 jobs in higher education, this site lists administrative and staff, executive, faculty, and part-time/adjunct positions. The service is free for candidates searching for a position, while there is a charge for institutions to post their jobs.

Independent Educational Service

http://www.ies-search.org/

The IES is a search firm for schools looking for new and experienced teachers. The school pays the fee. You can apply online, too!

jobs.com

http://www.jobs.com

In addition to having hundreds of thousands of jobs, and letting you manage your career search, jobs.com also offers unique features such as online career fairs. There are also articles, salary information, and testimonials from actual employees about their place of work.

JobWeb

http://www.jobweb.com

JobWeb is not a jobs search engine. Instead, they offer job seekers articles and assistance on interviews, resumes and cover letters, career tales from the real world and quick tips on your career quest. There is also a forum where you can talk with a career service expert.

K-12jobs.com

http://www.k12jobs.com

In addition to many K-12 faculty positions, K-12jobs.com also offers lists of job fairs, information and links to state licensure/certification, and more.

Monster.com

http://www.monster.com

Another huge job site with hundreds of thousands of jobs (of course, not all of them are in Education). Be sure to visit their Career Center, featuring resume assistance, cover letter examples, and interview resources (including a virtual interview).

NationJob – Education Jobs Page

http://www.nationjob.com/education/

Part of the NationJob Network, this site has a very large list of education-related jobs. Unfortunately, it is currently only available as one large list with no filtering or searching. Still, they seem to have more job postings that most of the other sites listed here.

National Council of Teachers of English Job List

http://www.ncte.org/classifieds

The NCTE offers a jobs database with positions in the fields of Language Arts, Literacy, Composition, Literature, English as a Second Language, Administration and Related Positions. You can also post your resume to the database.

National Council of Teachers of Mathematics Jobs Online

http://www.nctm.org/classifieds/jobsonline/

This jobs database, from the NCTM, mostly contains positions in higher education although there are usually some K-12 positions listed. NCTM members may also post their resume online.

National Teacher Recruitment Clearinghouse

http://www.recruitingteachers.org/

Instead of just searching for a job posting, why not search for a job bank? The NTRC offers a database of job banks, categorized by location. That's not all, though. This site has a lot of information on all aspects of the career search. Definitely one of the better career resource sites.

Peterson's Education Center

http://www.petersons.com

The education megasite also offers career search information, links to a jobs database, and feature articles on everything from preparing a portfolio to promises and pitfalls for job hunters on the web.

Resume Tutor

http://www1.umn.edu/ohr/ecep/resume/

An online service from the University of Minnesota, this site walks you step-by-step through the resume creation process. It won't save you any time but you will have a better chance of finishing with a quality resume.

Resume Magic

http://www.liglobal.com/b_c/career/res.html

A professional resume writer offers an article full of useful information on writing an effective resume. Samples of resumes are listed as well as a long list of links to other career-related websites.

State Employment Clearinghouses

http://www.special-ed-careers.org/educator_resources/state_clearinghouses.html

Most states have a site that lists job positions submitted by local employers. This page has links to all of the states' jobs websites.

Teacher Job Links

http://www.geocities.com/Athens/Forum/2080/

A mega-site of links to other sites. Choose a location on the "State by State" page and you'll get a page of links to many school district jobs pages. While not complete (they do not list every district in a state) this is still a very useful job search tool.

Teachers @ Work

http://www.teachersatwork.com/

Another teacher-only job database, this one also allows you to post your resume and have it viewed by subscribing school districts.

Teachers Helping Teachers with Teaching Exchanges

http://www.angelfire.com/ca/zael/

More than 20,000 teachers and their families went on a teaching exchange last year, according to this site. If you are interested in switching places with another teacher for a semester or two, this site is a must-see. There is information on exchanges, testimonials from those who have taken the plunge, and links to related sites.

WantToTeach.com

http://www.wanttoteach.com/

Another meta-site with links to other education-related job sites. This one is nicely organized by state and offers postings not found on other sites.

Child Development

A Child's Development Calendar

http://www.vtnea.org/vtnea14.htm

This is a good site that covers the basics of children's development, with information on the stages of the Observer, Toucher, Mover, Builder, Super Helper, Butterfly, Questioner, Expert, and Preschooler.

Billy Bear's Playground

http://www.billybear4kids.com/

There are many things here for the early childhood teacher (and her/his students). For the teacher, check out the clipart, free activity sheets, online lessons, and free downloadable software. For the students, there are online games, stories, and more. Very good site.

Center for the Improvement of Early Reading Achievement

http://www.ciera.org

CIERA's mission is to improve reading achievement by generating and disseminating theoretical, empirical, and practical solutions to persistent problems in the teaching and learning of early reading. The site offers many full-length articles and a good collection of reading-related links.

Child Care Aware

http://www.childcareaware.org/

Child Care Aware is a nonprofit initiative that serves as a directory for child care organizations and providers in the United States. You can search for a provider near you in just a few clicks. There are also tips for finding good care and avoiding bad providers.

Child Study.net

http://childstudy.net

This informative site presents a very detailed tutorial that covers child development month-by-month. Included in the tutorial are developmental milestones as well as comparisons to Freud's, Mahler's, and Erickson's theories. The site also offers a mailing list.

Culturally & Linguistically Appropriate Services – Early Childhood Research Institute

http://clas.uiuc.edu/

The CLAS Institute collects and describes early childhood/early intervention resources, and offer hundreds of pertinent articles, as well as video clips and links to other related sites.

Division for Early Childhood

http://www.dec-sped.org/

This division from the Council for Exceptional Children works with or on the behalf of children with special needs (birth – 8). This site offers membership information, news on conferences and meetings, and a job board.

Early Childhood Educator

http://www.edpsych.com/

For teachers, parents, and directors, Early Childhood Educator features articles on topics such as classroom management, a mailing list, and a well-designed resource section.

Early Childhood Educators' and Family Web Corner

http://users.sgi.net/~cokids/

This site may be the best meta-site on early childhood development. Links to other sites are listed by category and easy to find. The Teachers Pages section contains many links to sites useful for research.

Early Childhood Research & Practice

http://ecrp.uiuc.edu/

This is an online journal with articles on research devoted to the development, care, and education of young children. The articles from the six extant volumes are available in full-text form.

Early Childhood Today

http://teacher.scholastic.com/products/ect.htm

From Scholastic, the online version of the magazine. Many articles are available in full-text. Additionally, there is a section for receiving expert advice on development, information about conferences, activity plans, nutritional information, and more. Very good site.

Earlychildhood.com

http://www.earlychildhood.com/

Make no mistake, this is a commercial site (which means they want to sell you stuff). Still, there are many great resources here, including Sharing Boards (discussion forums), many articles about childhood development, and a good links section.

ECD Resource Map

http://www.worldbank.org/children/basics/sites.htm

The World Bank has folded all of their early childhood sites into this page, which offers a wealth of Internet resources on childhood development.

Eric Clearinghouse on Elementary and Early Childhood Education

http://www.ericeece.org/

The ERIC Clearinghouse offers publications and articles (most are abstracts, some full-text), links to other related websites, discussion groups, and more. Perhaps the most useful area is the AskERIC section, that allows you to email a question to an expert and receive an answer usually within 2 workdays.

Future of Children

http://www.futureofchildren.org/

From the David and Lucile Packard Foundation, this semi-annual report serves to disseminate information relating to the well-being of children. All of the articles in the report are available in full.

I Am Your Child

http://www.iamyourchild.org/

This organization seeks to make early childhood development a top priority for the United States. They sponsor research and educational programs. The site offers information for parents on child development.

Idea Box

http://www.theideabox.com/

Ideabox.com offers many ideas for the early childhood teacher. Ideas are grouped by activity, season, games, music and songs, recipes, and crafts. This site is slow and heavily commercialized but the ideas are worth a visit.

Kinder Korner

http://www.kinderkorner.com/

Kinder Korner is a website for teachers of grades pre-K through 2 maintained by Victoria Smith, a teacher in California. There are many complete units and themes available, as well as back to school ideas and much more. New themes for each part of the year are posted monthly.

Little Explorer Picture Dictionary

http://www.enchantedlearning.com/Dictionary.html

With more than 2,000 definitions, this dictionary is great for young children. Each word comes with a picture (you can even color some of them) and a complete definition. Most words also have a link to a related website.

Mother Goose Rebus Rhymes

http://www.enchantedlearning.com/Rhymes.html

Familiar rhymes with pictures. This site should be visited by teachers with their students. The rhymes are presented page by page, with illustrations, so they can be read by many students gathered around a monitor (or by everyone if projected on a screen).

Mr. Roger's Neighborhood

http://www.pbs.org/rogers/

Even though America's favorite neighbor passed away in 2003, his online presence continues. The web companion to the long-lived television show features online games for kids, information about the show, and songs sung by Mr. Rogers, with lyrics.

National Head Start Association

http://www.nhsa.org/

The NHSA provides a national forum for the continued enhancement of Head Start services for poor children ages 0 to 5, and their families. On this site there is information on NHSA publications, sponsored research, scheduled meetings and events, and more.

National Network for Child Care – Child Development

http://www.nncc.org

The Information Station section of the NNCC's site offers a great child development database featuring article, resources, and links on Assessment, Child Development, Literacy and many more. This is one of the best Child Development sites.

Perpetual Preschool

http://www.perpetualpreschool.com

A very good site that contains many teacher resources. The themes section, submitted by users of the site, is a particular standout. Other sections are devoted to learning centers, curriculum, teaching tips, and professional development.

Preschool Education

http://preschooleducation.com

This site offers many resources for teachers, organized in "classrooms" like Dramatic Play and Incentives. There are also articles, message boards, and mailing lists. The site's biggest drawback is its commercialization and use of irritating pop-up advertisements. Be patient if you visit here.

Preschool By Stormie

http://www.preschoolbystormie.com/

This is a nice site that makes it easy to access its useful resources. There are many tips for the preschool teacher on all facets of teaching. Teachers will also find monthly curriculums, activities, a children's gallery, and more.

ReadyWeb

http://readyweb.crc.uiuc.edu/

An online resource for educators, ReadyWeb maintains a collection of resources on school readiness. The site offers many research articles for educators, though some of the links are broken. There are also articles and resources for parents.

Sesame Workshop

http://www.ctw.org/

From the Children's Television Workshop, the Sesame Workshop offers games for the preschooler featuring the beloved Sesame Street characters. The Workshop also offers free printables for teachers and information for parents. There's even a section where children can e-mail their favorite character and receive a personalized reply.

Wee Family Pages

http://millennium.fortunecity.com/plumpton/304/home.html

Another site for early childhood teachers that features hundreds of activity ideas. All activities are presented in a simple index and many come with very complete instructions.

World of Kindergartens

http://www.coe.iup.edu/worldofkindergarten/

If you need ideas for activities, World of Kindergarten features hundreds, all organized simply in an alphabetical index. Many subjects are provided with pictures, related websites, songs and poems, recipes, and a list of books.

Classroom and
Behavior Management

50 Tips on Classroom Management for ADD

http://www.enteract.com/~peregrin/add/50clas.html

This well-written and easy-to-read paper written by Dr. Ned Hallowell details strategies teachers can use to manage the classroom effectively for students with ADD.

101 Things You Can Do the First Three Weeks of Class

http://www.udel.edu/cte/101things.htm

From the Center for Teaching Effectiveness, a list of things teachers can do to help get their year off to a successful start. This lists deals with transitions, support, attention, active learning, community building and more.

Athena - Classroom Management

http://vathena.arc.nasa.gov/project/teacher/manage/

Funded by NASA, Athena attempts to teach the earth sciences. This particular section of their website deals with issues of classroom management as it relates to computer usage (sharing of computers, acceptable use policies, keeping track of student Internet usage, etc.).

Behavior Home Page

http://www.state.ky.us/agencies/behave/homepage.html

From the Kentucky Department of Education, this site provides information on managing classroom behavior and tips and strategies for effective interventions.

CanTeach - Classroom Management Discipline & Organization

http://www.track0.com/canteach/elementary/classman.html

This section of the CanTeach site offers ways to encourage good behavior, a list of reward ideas, things to do when the seatwork is done, lists of theme ideas, and some examples of school and class pledges.

Center for Performance Technology - Behavior

http://cpt.fsu.edu/tree/behavior.html

This site features journal articles pertaining to behavior. Best among them may be "Guideline for Establishing and Maintaining Token Economies."

Classroom Discipline Resources

http://7-12educators.miningco.com/msub49.htm

From About.com, a long list of Internet sites related to classroom discipline. A good resource that is usually up-to-date.

Classroom Management

http://www.temple.edu/CETP/temple_teach/cm-intro.html

From the University of Temple, this site was created for their teacher education students. It offers tips for managing classroom space, enacting routines, standards of conduct, knowing your students, and setting up instruction.

Classroom Management (Teachers Helping Teachers)

http://www.pacificnet.net/~mandel/ClassroomManagement.html

Many suggestions from practicing teachers on different methods of classroom management and how to implement them. Applicable to all grades.

Classroom Management Concepts

http://www.osr.state.ga.us/bestprac/class/clmgt_toc.htm

A six-part online booklet that details the concepts of classroom management in kindergartens and how to make those concepts work in the real world.

Classroom Management – FLTEACH FAQ

http://www.cortland.edu/flteach/FAQ/FAQ-Classroom-Management.html

Suggestions from foreign language teachers for the start of class, transitions, seating charts, student motivation, student contracts, and more can be found here. Useful for any classroom.

Classroom Management from Teachnet.com

http://www.teachnet.com/how-to/manage

Articles on classroom management dealing with behavior and discipline. Learn how to implement a classroom "court," what you can do to increase attendance, and how to contract for grades and behavior.

Classroom Management Plan

http://www.geom.umn.edu/~dwiggins/plan.html

A very detailed classroom management from Dave Wiggins at the University of Minnesota. The plan divided is into two parts: preventive discipline, and supportive and corrective discipline.

Classroom Management Special Education

http://www.pacificnet.net/~mandel/SpecialEducation.html

Many suggestions from practicing teachers (from the Teachers Helping Teachers site) detail different methods of classroom management and how to implement them. Applicable to all grades.

Consistency Management and Cooperative Discipline

http://www.coe.uh.edu/~freiberg/cm/index3.html

Consistency Management and Cooperative Discipline has, at its core, a shared responsibility for learning and classroom organizations. This website explains (and extols) the CMCD approach.

Dr. Mac's Amazing Behavior Management Advice Site

http://maxweber.hunter.cuny.edu/pub/eres/EDSPC715_MCINTYRE/715HomePage.html

The address may be hard to remember, but you'll be glad you typed it when you see what this site has to deliver. One of the best classroom management sites, Dr. Mac offers tips on managing student behavior, how-to articles, a behavior management primer, cartoons, resources (including related links), and more.

ERIC Database

http://www.eric.ed.gov/

If you're looking for articles on classroom management, try the ERIC database first. On the homepage look for the Search ERIC Database tab. Type 'classroom management' in the search box and click the Search button to see a long list of ERIC digests (summaries of articles) about classroom management.

Filling the Toolbox

http://www.fno.org/toolbox.html

An article that appeared in the From Now On journal, this explains a classroom strategy that changes the management style in the classroom, one that moves from teacher-centered to learner-centered.

Gentle Teaching

http://www.gentleteaching.nl/

Gentle Teaching focuses on interdependence and teaching others to feel safe. This page explains the theory behind Gentle Teaching and its eight basic values.

Honor Level System

http://www.honorlevel.com

This site presents The Honor Level System: Discipline by Design, a five-part series that details the benefits of the honor level system and how a teacher would implement it in the classroom. Also included are the 11 techniques for better classroom discipline.

Kim's Korner for Teacher Talk – Ideas for Many Areas of Classroom Management

http://www.angelfire.com/ks/teachme/classmanagement.html

If you need help in getting organized, a visit to this site may be a good first step. There are many useful ideas to help you prepare the physical space of your classroom as well as improve the procedures you employ. The site also offers more information in the areas of rewards, rules, and more.

Innovative Classroom - Classroom Management

http://www.theteachersguide.com/ClassManagement.htm

Tips and strategies for managing your classroom, including hundreds of organizational tips and activity ideas. The other sections of the site, including the Teaching Toolbox and Lesson Plan areas, are equally useful.

Managing Inappropriate Behavior in the Classroom

http://www.ed.gov/databases/ERIC_Digests/ed371506.html

From an ERIC Digest written by the Council for Exceptional Children, a question/answer type document about classroom management strategies.

Organization and Management of the Classroom

http://para.unl.edu/para/Organization/Intro.html

Part of a website for paraprofessionals, this is a chapter of an online book that covers classroom organization, rules and procedures, information on how to work with small groups, as well as lessons, activities, and even tests. Also visit Unit 5, which covers behavior management.

Positive Behavioral Interventions and Supports

http://www.ideapractices.org/resources/files/pbis.pdf

This article from the U. S. Office of Special Education Programs outlines the Positive Behavioral Intervention and Support process used with both special needs and mainstream children. Information on where to go for more information is also provided.

Positive Reinforcement: A Self-Instructional Exercise

http://psych.athabascau.ca/html/prtut/reinpair.htm

This exercise attempts to teach the concept of positive reinforcement by using examples, non-examples, and analysis. Very informative.

Schoolwide and Classroom Discipline

http://www.nwrel.org/scpd/sirs/5/cu9.html

This very useful report consolidates the findings of more than 60 other research articles about classroom management. It summarizes the findings, and describes what works and what doesn't, in the areas of schoolwide discipline, classroom management, teacher training in classroom management, discipline and more. You can find more articles on behavior management through their search engine at http://www.nwrel.org

ProTeacher! Behavior Management and Positive Discipline Plans and Strategies for Elementary School

http://www.proteacher.com/030001.shtml

Search the archives for ideas from elementary teachers for any topic, including classroom management and discipline. Or, ask questions, share ideas, or simply vent your frustrations on one of 30 discussion boards.

Teacher Talk

http://education.indiana.edu/cas/tt/v1i2/table.html

For secondary teachers, a volume of Teacher Talk devoted to classroom management. Topics include different management styles, a classroom management profile exercise, and teachers' answers to the question, "How can beginning teachers show they are caring while maintaining order in the classroom?'

Teacher's Encyclopedia of Behavior Management

http://www.state.ky.us/agencies/behave/bi/encyndex.html

Two problem behaviors: aggression (verbal and/or physical) and chaos (classroom out of control). Plans to intervene and correct the behaviors are addressed here by Dr. Randall Sprick. There are also articles on behavioral interventions and law.

Teaching Help

http://www.foothill.net/~moorek/

Written by an experienced teacher, this website offers tips on several classroom management issues, like transitions, time on task, and management systems. Very well written.

Time Out Procedures

http://www.state.ky.us/agencies/behave/bi/TO.html

A very good article that explains the objectives of Time Out, the rationale behind its use, how it should be implemented, how it could be abused, an evaluation checklist, and more.

What Is Your Classroom Management Profile?

http://education.indiana.edu/cas/tt/v1i2/what.html

Take this very interesting online quiz that uses your responses to determine whether your style is authoritarian, authoritative, laissez-faire, or indifferent. Information is also provided about each of the different styles.

Works4Me

http://www.nea.org/helpfrom/growing/works4me/library.html

This site includes information on classroom management techniques as well as tips on getting organized, using technology, and content delivery. From the NEA. Very good resource.

Writing Effective Behavior Plans

http://www.specialedjobs.com/behaviorplan.html

A short article detailing reasons that behavior plans sometimes fail and suggestions for writing effective plans.

You Can Handle Them All

http://www.disciplinehelp.com

This is a very good site. 117 different misbehaviors, like "The Apathetic," are listed. For each one, the site gives a set of descriptors, lists the effects this type of student can have on others, suggests actions for dealing with the behavior, and describes common errors in managing the behavior. A discussion board, a weekly tip-of-the-week e-mail, and a "behavior of the day" rounds out this site.

Diversity in the Classroom

African-American Mosaic

http://lcWeb.loc.gov/exhibits/african/intro.html

From the Library of Congress comes an online exhibition that explores the study of black history and culture. There are sections on colonization, abolition, and migration that feature primary works while the WPA sections includes ex-slave narratives as well as maps and original documents.

Africana.com

http://www.africana.com

This may be the best site devoted to African and African-American history and culture. Billed as The Gateway to the Black World, this encyclopedic site covers hundreds of topics and offers informative articles, multimedia presentations, and community rooms.

America's Life Histories—Manuscripts from the Federal Writer's Project 1936-1940

http://lcWeb2.loc.gov/ammem/wpaintro/wpahome.html

The Federal Writer's Project was a Depression-era government plan that put writers to work chronicling the history of the country in the words of those who lived it. This site contains thousands of interviews done for this project. You'll need the QuickTime player to view the original pages.

An End to Intolerance

http://www.iearn.org/hgp/aeti/student-magazine.html

An End to Intolerance is an annual magazine produced by students around the world. Each issue focuses on an aspect of the Holocaust. All of the articles from the issues of 1993 to 2002 are online.

Ask Asia

http://www.askasia.org/

A portal for websites about Asia, Ask Asia now offers an expanded Teachers Resources section that contains lessons plans, maps, photographs, and much more. The Students section contains articles and maps and even a section on origami. This site continues to expand its content and has become a must-visit for those interested in Asia.

Kids' Quest on Disability and Health

http://funrsc.fairfield.edu/~jfleitas/contents.html

This site is dedicated to sensitizing children to what it's like to grow up with a medical problem. There are sections for kids, teens, and adults.

Center for Multilingual Multicultural Research

http://www.usc.edu/dept/education/CMMR/

From the University of Southern California, the CMMR offers current news, a live chat room and more. Highlight of the site are the categorical lists of links to other Internet resources. If you are looking for research materials, this is a very good place to begin your search.

Center for World Indigenous Studies

http://www.cwis.org

The goal of the Center for World Indigenous Studies is to give access to peoples' ideas in order to reduce the possibility of conflict and increase understanding. Information on traditional healing, employment resources and more.

Chinese Historical and Cultural Project

http://www.chcp.org/

Founded in Santa Clara, California, the CHCP website offers a very good Virtual Museum and Virtual Library section that features information on Chinese music, customs, festivals, history in the U.S., arts, and more.

CMMR – Bilingual/ESL/Multicultural Education Resources

http://www-bcf.usc.edu/~cmmr/BEResources.html

This Web site points pre-kindergarten to higher education teachers to commercial and non-commercial sources for multicultural and bilingual/ESL education information, articles, professional development resources, family resources, and much more.

Cultural Arts Resources for Teachers and Students

http://www.carts.org

Providing traditional arts and folklore resources for teachers and students, CARTS has established a deep site full of useful information. The Regional Resources section is the highlight of the site.

Culture-Quest World Tour

http://www.ipl.org/div/kidspace/cquest

This site is part of the Internet Public Library. Students can learn about featured countries, their holidays, recipes, games, etc. Not all countries are featured, however, and this is the major drawback to this site. Still, it is a good resource for culture exploration.

Distinguished Women of Past and Present

http://www.distinguishedwomen.com/

Containing biographies of women who made cultural and historical contributions. You can search by name or browse through the subject list. Very good site.

Diversity in the Classroom

http://www.princeton.edu/~djbutler/ditclink.htm

This page is a collection of well-annotated links to diversity articles and web pages around the Internet. A well-represented cross section of issues are represented and the articles all make for illuminating reading.

Education First: Black History Activities

http://www.kn.pacbell.com/wired/BHM/AfroAm.html

Six websites on African-American history (they also serve as examples on how to integrate the web and videoconferencing into the classroom). Site titles: Black History Hotlist, Black History Past to Present (interactive treasure hunt), Sampling African America, a Webquest on the Little Rock 9, and Tuskegee Tragedy. There are also well-annotated links to other quality resources.

Encyclopedia Britannica Guide to Black History

http://blackhistory.eb.com/

A great site from Britannica.com featuring a timeline, many informative articles and biographies, audio and video clips of important moments in black history, and a very good related links section. A well-designed and attractive site.

Equity and Cultural Diversity

http://eric-Web.tc.columbia.edu/equity

This site deals with educational equity and cultural diversity in the classroom. If offers information on conferences, publications, parental resources, ERIC/CUE Digests, Monographs, and Information Alerts, and more good research resources.,

ESL Activities for Students

http://grove.ufl.edu/~ktrickel/activity.html

Thematic units that incorporate native listening materials in the RealAudio format. Probably better suited for secondary teachers/students.

ESL Resource Center

http://eslus.com/eslcenter.htm

The center features lessons created for students studying at INTERLINK Language Centers. There is also a great set of links to other related resources on the web and even a Hangman game!

Ethnologue, Languages of the World

http://www.ethnologue.com

Ethnologue offers information on the many languages spoken throughout the world. It includes languages of special interest, the spatial distribution of language and the number of speakers of the top 100 languages. Did you know that there are more than 170 languages spoken in the United States? You'll learn that and much more at this site.

Exploring Ancient World Cultures

http://eawc.evansville.edu/

This site, for high school students, offers information on the ancient cultures in India, Egypt, China, Greece, Rome, Europe, and other places. Each section is heavily annotated and features informative articles.

Feminist Chronicles

http://www.feminist.org/research/chronicles/chronicl.html

Exploring the later history of the women's movement, the Feminist Chronicles offers in-depth articles, primary documents, and a chronological list of important events in the history of the movement.

Foreign Language Links

http://www.puhsd.k12.ca.us/placer/pages/foreign_library.html

A big site that features categorized lists of links to many different foreign language pages on the Web (primarily Spanish, German, and French), as well as international newspapers and magazines.

History of the Cherokee

http://cherokeehistory.com

A good site that explains history as seen by the Cherokee. It includes Cherokee beliefs on creation, their legends, and genealogy. The highlight of the site may be the Images and Maps section.

Intercultural E-Mail Classroom Connections

http://www.iecc.org/

The IECC (Intercultural E-Mail Classroom Connections) mailing lists are provided by St. Olaf College as a free service to help teachers and classes link with partners in other countries and cultures for e-mail, classroom pen pals, and project exchanges. It currently boasts more than 7,500 users in 82 countries.

Interesting Jewish Resource on the Internet

http://www.pacificnet.net/~mandel/jewish.html

This site features annotated links to Jewish resources on the web. Categories include College Life, Culture, General Information, Holocaust, Israel, Kashrut, Text Study, and Women.

K–12 Electronic Guide for African Resources on the Internet

http://www.sas.upenn.edu/African_Studies/Home_Page/AFR_GIDE.html

The aim of this guide is to assist K–12 teachers, librarians, and students in locating online resources on Africa that can be used in the classroom for research and studies. This guide summarizes some relevant materials for K-12 uses available on the African Studies WWW.

Let's Go!: Around the World

http://www.ccph.com

Let's Go combines cultures in other parts of the world with language arts instruction in your classroom. There are online field trips to the Amazon, East Africa, and other places as well as an International Art Exchange and an Adopt a School program. The Teacher's Resource section is worth a look, too.

Martin Luther King, Jr.

http://seattletimes.nwsource.com/mlk/

From the Seattle Times, this in-depth look at the life and impact of Martin Luther King, Jr. is full of details and descriptions. Included are sound clips of the "I Have A Dream" and "Promised Land" speeches—a very good site.

Martin Luther King, Jr. Papers Project

http://www.stanford.edu/group/King/

A comprehensive site that offers papers written by Dr. Martin Luther King Jr. and secondary documents about his life. Contains his Nobel Prize acceptance speech, the address at the March on Washington for Jobs and Freedom, and much more.

Mathematicians of the African Diaspora

http://www.math.buffalo.edu/mad/

This is an excellent website that provides biographical information on 400 black mathematicians. There is also information on black computer scientists, a good timeline of math, and more than 40 special articles, posters, and exhibits.

Mexico for Kids

http://www.elbalero.gob.mx/index_kids.html

Available in Spanish, Italian, French, and English, Mexico for Kids is an interactive website that explores the history, geography, government, and culture of Mexico. The site also offers some special features, such as create your own stationery and a picture submission section. Very good site.

Multicultural Pavilion

http://curry.edschool.virginia.edu/go/multicultural/

The Multiculturalism Pavilion provides resources for educators, students and activists to explore and discuss multicultural education and to facilitate opportunities for educators to work toward self-awareness and development. They offer teaching tools, original papers, a Listserv, a discussion forum, and so much more.

Multicultural Perspectives in Mathematics Education

http://jwilson.coe.uga.edu/DEPT/Multicultural/MathEd.html

This site is maintained by the University of Georgia's Department of Mathematics and serves as a repository for information about multiculturalism in mathematics. Resources include an annotated bibliography of multicultural issues in mathematics, a list of relevant dissertations, and a good list of links.

National Civil Rights Museum

http://www.civilrightsmuseum.org/

The National Civil Rights Museum presents a virtual tour of the civil rights movement in the 1960s. The online exhibits are informative and present information on the quest for civil rights in America.

National Women's History Project

http://www.nwhp.org/

Recognizing and celebrating women's accomplishments, the NWHP provides resources for learning more about women's history. The highlight of the site is their list of links, but there are also lists of related museums, organizations, and performers by state.

Native American Lore Index

http://www.ilhawaii.net/~stony/loreindx.html

Native American lore from many tribes. There are more than 130 stories collected from tribes across Turtle Island. Some of the stories may not be for all listeners.

Native Web

http://www.nativeweb.org/

Featuring resources for indigenous cultures around the world, Native Web is a huge repository of information on indigenous cultures. It offers more than 3,000 links to other sites, communities, books and music, and much more.

Six Paths to China

http://www.kn.pacbell.com/wired/China/

Originally created as a way to integrate the Web into classroom learning, the product of this exercise is a great resource on China. There's a page of annotated proverbs, a Webquest, and a Treasure Hunt.

Slave Voices

http://odyssey.lib.duke.edu/slavery/

From the Special Collections Library of Duke University, the story of slavery is retold with the documents of the period. Bills of sale, newspaper advertisements, diaries, etc., are reproduced and interpreted— a very good site.

Stories of the Dreaming

http://www.dreamtime.net.au/main.htm

Stories of the Dreaming features stories from the indigenous peoples of Australia presented in a very nice design. The stories are presented as text, audio, and video, so they can be used with nonreaders and readers alike. This site is an excellent use of the Web.

Teaching Tolerance

http://www.splcenter.org/teachingtolerance/tt-index.html

Created by the Southern Poverty Law Center, Teaching Tolerance is dedicated to assisting teachers to help foster equity, respect, and understanding in the classroom. The site offers classroom activities and resources, teaching tools, and information on grants.

World Info Zone

http://www.worldinfozone.com/

This site (formerly the WTech Gateway) spotlights different countries and areas of the world in order to bring about more understanding among the different peoples on the globe. Each country has hyperlinked information on many various subjects. The site features more than 2,000 external hyperlinks to sites that have been checked for content.

Early Childhood

Activity Idea Place

http://www.123child.com

Over 800 different activities for young children, categorized by Animals, Seasons and Holidays, and Other/Misc. The descriptions for each activity are very concise.

BBC Parenting

http://www.bbc.co.uk/parenting/your_kids/

In addition to producing quality television, the BBC is into parenting. Specifically, its parenting section of the website offers tons of resources on your child and school, including preparing for nursery or elementary school, information on developmental stages, and much more.

ChildFun.com

http://www.childfun.com/themes/school.shtml

The address above links to a section of the ChildFun.com site that has a collection of links on preparing your child for school. Resources include a Kindergarten Readiness Checklist, helping your child become a better reader, and a very informative Ask the Teacher section.

Developmentally Appropriate Practice in Early Childhood Education

http://www.ed.psu.edu/k-12/edpgs/su96/ece/dap1.html

A small clearinghouse to other Developmentally Appropriate Practice (DAP) websites. This site features links to sites about the theories that influence DAP and curricular issues and applications.

Early Child Development

http://www.worldbank.org/children/

From the World Bank, a collection of resources including online journals (Child Welfare, Early Childhood Today), reports on early childhood research, including the efficacy of Head Start programs, and more.

Early Childhood Care and Development

http://www.ecdgroup.com/

This site offers a plethora of articles on early childhood development. There is an international focus here, with issues addressed that are not limited to the United States. This is an excellent site.

Early Childhood Education Online

http://www.ume.maine.edu/ECEOL-L/

There are two primary sections to this site. One is a Listserv you can join to share support and information with others. The other section offers web resources on diversity, developmental guidelines, observation and assessment, and curriculum and other issues.

ECE Web Guide

http://www.myscschools.com/offices/ece/

Acting as a clearinghouse of sorts for all things early childhood, the ECE Web Guide offers a well-categorized collection of links to early childhood-related sites on the web. The site does suffer from the irritating use of pop-up ads and annoying flashing banners.

Edu.Puppy.com

http://www.edupuppy.com/

If you're having a difficult time finding an early childhood website (preschool–grade 2), this is the place to visit. More than 40 categories, hundreds of subcategories, and thousands and thousands of sites (maybe a few too many, since it is difficult to tell what's good and what isn't until you visit them—a ranking system would be helpful). Still, a great site.

Gayle's Preschool Rainbow

http://www.preschoolrainbow.org/

The Preschool Rainbow is a collection of hundreds of activity ideas for teachers of young children. The site is nicely categorized by theme and is made more valuable by the comments of teachers who have implemented the activity in their classrooms.

Getting Young Children Ready to Learn

http://www.humsci.auburn.edu/parent/ready/paus1.htm

The content of this site is very good—how to get students ready to learn by developing language abilities, self-control, social skills. The site's presentation could use some work since you'll be paging through shots of a scanned article.

Home School Advisor

http://www.hsadvisor.com/

If you're thinking about home schooling but don't know where to start, visit this site. Their advice section answers questions that those new to home schooling often ask. The site also has an excellent list of typical courses of study for preschool–grade 12 as well as links to online resources and items for purchase.

National Network for Child Care

http://www.nncc.org/Child.Dev/child.dev.page.html

A great place to find information on early childhood, this site from the NNCC offers lesson ideas for kids from infancy to age 12. There is also a lot of information on developmental milestones.

Early Childhood and Parenting Collaborative Information Technology Group (ECAP/ITG)

http://ecap.crc.uiuc.edu/info/

This is the place to go if you are an early childhood educator looking for Internet-based articles, experts to help you find resources, Web design help, online chat rooms or listservs, and much more. ECAP/ITG is staffed by writers, editors, web designers, and librarians ready to help you find the online resources you need.

Preschool Lesson Plans

http://lessonplanz.com/Lesson_Plans/Language_Arts/_ _ _Preschool/

This section of the LessonPlanz.com site offers more than 50 lesson plans for young children in the areas of alphabet, phonemic awareness, centers and more.

Preschool Resources – Everything Preschool

http://www.everythingpreschool.com/

Everything Preschool has lesson plans, thematic curriculum, coloring pages, toy, software, and book reviews, as well as message boards for the early childhood educator. A great resource for the preschool teacher.

Teacher Vision

http://www.teachervision.com/tv/

The Lesson Plan section of Teacher Vision offers links to more than 200 plans for pre-K children. Make sure you check out their great collection of printables, too.

Zero to Three

http://www.zerotothree.org/

The parents' section of this site contains many useful articles on beginning literacy, early routines that promote later success in school, and more. The professionals' section features information on training and policy initiatives. Be sure to check out the Brain Wonders section, which explores how to help babies and toddlers grow and develop.

Education Laws, Regulations, and Standards

Americans with Disabilities Act Document Center

http://www.jan.wvu.edu/links/adalinks.htm

This site features the full text copy of the American with Disabilities Act as well as questions and answers about the Act. It also offers a good list of links to other related websites.

Content Knowledge

http://www.mcrel.org/standards-benchmarks/

The MCREL Standards Database is a very complete consolidation of more than 100 national and state-level documents that address standards and benchmarks at the K-12 level.

Developing Educational Standards

http://edstandards.org/Standards.html

This very extensive site catalogues nationwide educational standards, initiatives, and curriculum framework documents. Standards are presented by subject area and by state.

EdLaw

http://www.edlaw.net

Laws and other documents related to education are contained at this very extensive site. The site presents full-text copies of IDEA Regulations, the Rehabilitation Act of 1973, and the Family Educational Rights and Privacy Act.

Education Law Association

http://www.educationlaw.org/

The Education Law Association promotes interest in and understanding of the legal framework of education and the rights of students, parents, school boards and school employees. The site offers membership information, details on upcoming conferences, and a catalog of current publications.

Education Law Center

http://www.edlawcenter.org/

The ELC promotes school reform by enforcing and expanding the rights of individual students. The site contains articles on early childhood, school facilities, and more.

IDEA 97

http://www.ed.gov/offices/OSERS/Policy/IDEA

From the Office of Special Education and Rehabilitative Services, information on the Individuals with Disabilities Education Act, including 1997 amendments.

National Center for Research on Evaluation, Standards, and Student Testing

http://cresst96.cse.ucla.edu

CREST conducts research on K-12 educational testing. They have posted all of their reports, newsletters, assessments, rubrics, and more online. There is also a useful Ask the Expert section where you can ask questions about assessment and educational reform and receive answers from one of the members of the CREST team.

National Center on Educational Outcomes

http://www.coled.umn.edu/NCEO/

The NCEO provides national leadership in the identification of outcomes and indicators to monitor educational results for all students. This website provides online full-text reports from the NCEO

National Education Goals Panel

http://www.negp.gov

This site provides information on the eight national goals as described by the Congress and state governors. Areas include: progress reports, ready to learn, school completion, math and literacy.

National Science Education Standards

http://www.nap.edu/readingroom/books/nses/html/

Find the standards providing specific guidelines on content, teaching, professional development, and assessment of science education programs and systems.

National Standards for Art Education

http://www.artteacherconnection.com/pages/standards.htm

This section of the Art Teacher Connection site makes the complete national standards for art education, developed by the Consortium of National Arts Education Associations and titled What Every Young American Should Know and Be Able to Do in the Arts, available online.

National Standards for Foreign Language Education

http://www.actfl.org/public/articles/details.cfm?id=33

The American Council on the Teaching of Foreign Languages hosts this page that offers information on the foreign language standards. You can read the executive summary online and other information about the standards but, inexplicably, it appears you'll have to send them $25 for the complete standards document.

National Standards for Math Education

http://www.nctm.org/standards/

From the National Council of Teachers of Mathematics, their proposed standards and goals for math education.

National Standards for Physical Education

http://www.ed.gov/databases/ERIC_Digests/ed406361.html

Information on the National Standards for Physical Education, as put forth by the National Association for Sport and Physical Education.

National Standards for Social Studies

http://www.ncss.org/standards/stitle.html

From the National Council for the Social Studies, their proposal for standards and goals in social studies education. This is just an excerpt; like the foreign language standards noted above, you have to pay for the full report.

No Child Left Behind

http://www.nclb.gov/

This is the home page for the No Child Left Behind Act, the latest attempt by the federal government to "reform" education. The site offers information on the legislation as well as details about its implementation and resources for parents and teachers.

National Standards for United States History

http://www.sscnet.ucla.edu/nchs/standards.html

At this site are the complete national standards for U.S. History for grades K–4 and 5–12 and the national standards for world history.

Thomas – Legislative Information on the Internet

http://thomas.loc.gov

This is one of the best websites. A free service from the Library of Congress, Thomas features an exhaustive list of federal and state laws, available in full as well as the Congressional Record. It even includes the constitutions and laws of other nations and hundreds of treaties and other international laws.

Wrightslaw - Special Education Law & Advocacy

http://www.wrightslaw.com/

This commercial site offers many resources for the educator, including a library full of informative articles about education and the law. The site also offers a free Special Ed Advocate Newsletter.

Funding Sources

Alfred P. Sloan Foundation

http://www.sloan.org

A very well-known source of grant and other funding opportunities, the Sloan Foundation awarded over $35 million in 1996 alone. Their five primary interests are 1. Science and Technology, 2. Standard of Living and Economic Performance, 3. Education and Careers in Science and Technology, 4. Selected National Issues, and 5. Civic Projects. This site contains all the information needed to apply for a grant.

AT&T Foundation

http://www.att.com/giving/

The AT&T Foundation offers grants in the areas of Education, Arts and Culture, and Civic and Community Service. Their website presents information about each program and guidelines for applications. It also features links to their other education initiatives, including the AT&T Learning Network (http://www.att.com/learningnetwork/) which offers many resources for teachers.

Bill and Melinda Gates Foundation

http://www.gatesfoundation.org/default.htm

The Gates Foundation's main education emphasis is the Teacher Leadership Project, which funds technology and training to teachers working with 5th through 7th graders. This website details their programs and gives contact information.

Carnegie Corporation of New York

http://www.carnegie.org

Although the Carnegie Corporation does not usually give grants to individuals (there are some exceptions), they do make many grants to academic institutions and other professional organizations. You'll find application information as well as details on recently funded grants (good way to see what the CC likes to fund).

College is Possible

http://www.collegeispossible.org

You probably already know that it's possible to go to college but some of your students might not. This resource guide, provided by the American Council for Education, presents information on preparing for college, choosing the right school, and, of course, paying for the privilege of attending. There is also a good section on adults returning to college.

Council for International Exchange of Scholars

http://www.iie.org/cies/

This site provides information on the Fulbright Scholar Competition. The Fulbright Program is designed, to "increase mutual understanding between the people of the United States and the people of other countries."

David and Lucile Packard Foundation

http://www.packard.org/

The David and Lucile Packard Foundation offers grants in several areas pertaining to education and educators, including children, families, and communities. The site provides application information.

Dos and Don'ts of Grant Writing

http://web.gisd.k12.mi.us/gisd/Dos_and_Donts_Chart.htm

This is a straight to the point list of what to do (and what not to do) when writing grants. Each section of the grant, including the cover letter, introduction, need, plan of operation, and budget, is covered.

FastAID

http://www.fastaid.com

Simple but very effective. Give them some information and they'll give you a list of scholarships that you are eligible for and instructions on how to apply. Best of all, it's free!

fastWEB.com

http://www.fastweb.com

Much like FastAID, this site uses information submitted by you to do a scholarship search from a database of more than 600,000 scholarships, loans, grants, etc, worth more than $1 billion (though you probably won't qualify for all of them!). They'll even help you write the letters!

FinAid

http://www.finaid.org

Vast site featuring dozens of financial aid categories. Includes useful aid calculators, information of financial aid scams and so much more that you have to visit the site to believe it.

Foundation Center

http://www.fdncenter.org

An online orientation to the grant-seeking process highlights this site. Also includes a comprehensive "User-Friendly Guide to Funding Research and Resources." Some of the sections of the site have recently required paid membership to access but this is still a worthwhile resource.

Getting Grants – Grant Writing School

http://granthelp.clarityconnect.com/school.htm

This is a free collection of lessons on how to write a grant. The lessons cover types of grants, sources of money, what funding sources look for in a grant, the necessary documentation, resource investigation, and writing the proposal.

Grant Opportunity Resources

http://www.kn.pacbell.com/wired/grants

A good collection of links on finding money and writing proposals. The best section is "Tools," a review of software that might make your grant writing proposal process easier.

Grants Net

http://www.grantsnet.org/

Grants Net is a tool for finding and exchanging information about federal grant programs. It is part of the much-publicized national movement toward providing government resources to the general public in a more accessible and meaningful manner.

GrantsWeb

http://www.srainternational.org/newweb/grantsweb/

A huge site with lots of information on grants and other funding opportunities from government and private organizations. Categories: Government Resources, Policy Information and Circulars, General Resources, Private Funding Resources, and Links.

Grantwriting Basics

http://www.megrants.org/grantwriting.html

If you've never written a grant before, this would be a good page to review. Jon Hardie describes the ins and outs of the grant process, how your proposal will be reviewed, and much more.

International Education Financial Aid

http://www.iefa.org

The IEFA offers resources for students wishing to finance study at overseas locations in keeping with their mission to promote international education. The site includes a searchable scholarship database.

International Research & Exchanges Board

http://www.irex.org

The IREX offers grant opportunities to domestic international students in many areas, including individual research opportunities and contemporary issues fellowships. Their programs are nicely categorized by region, country, and topic.

IRIS Funding Opportunities

http://carousel.lis.uiuc.edu/~iris/search.html

This searchable database of thousands includes grants in every area from agriculture to zoology. You can search by keyword, deadline date, or sponsor name. It is updated daily by the sponsors. There is also a section on upcoming deadlines.

Mr. Holland's Opus Foundation

http://www.mhopus.com/

The Mr. Holland's Opus Foundations partners with businesses, schools and communities to provide instruments to qualifying students and schools. This site provides grant information and applications.

National Association of Student Financial Aid Administrators (NASFAA)

http://www.nasfaa.org/ParentsStudents.asp?Tab=parentsStudents

The NASFAA is an organization of those institutions and people interested in the effective administration of student financial aid. It provides information to parents and students on the process of applying and paying for a college education. Direct your students to the helpful online forms.

National Science Foundation Funding Opportunities and Awards

http://www.nsf.gov/home/grants.htm

This section of the NSF's site is devoted to grant opportunities and provides a searchable database of grant opportunities and information on how to apply. Categories: Funding Opportunities, Proposal Preparation, Award Administration, Award Data, and Contracts.

Notices of Funding Availability

http://ocd.usda.gov/nofa.htm

Notices of Funding Availability (NOFAs) are notices that are issued each day by the federal government and printed in the Federal Register. This site lets you search for particular NOFAs based on keyword and agency.

Petersons.com - Financing Education

http://www.petersons.com/resources/finance.html

This website from Petersons offers a large amount of information on financing a college education. There are feature articles explaining financial aid and scholarships, and a scholarship search database.

Research Funding Opportunities and Administration (TRAM)

http://tram.east.asu.edu/

TRAM features a search engine for locating funding opportunities. It also maintains a set of grant application forms from various sources, standard agreements forms, and more.

Research Sponsors

http://www.cs.virginia.edu/research/sponsors.html

From the University of Virginia comes a very extensive list of governmental, public, and private organizations where funding can be obtained for educational projects. Government agencies, foundations and associations, and searchable grant databases are all well-represented.

Schoolgrants.org

http://www.schoolgrants.org

Featuring information on grant opportunities for K–12 schools, Schoolgrants.org is a good first-stop for grant seekers. The grant information is well-organized, and lists deadlines, eligibility requirements, program purpose, and links to the grant-givers' websites.

SMARTer Kids Foundation

http://www.smarterkids.org/

This private foundation offers grants that help educators purchase technology for their classroom or school. This site has complete information on all of their grant programs.

TAP: The Ada Project

http://www.cs.yale.edu/~tap/fellowships.html

From The Ada Project, a very good list of annotated links and contact addresses for fellowships, grants, and awards information.

TeachNet.org

http://www.teachnet.org

TeachNet.org offers updated information on grants and resources for teachers. They also offer teacher-designed projects and activities that incorporate technology.

Technology Grant Programs

http://www.ed.gov/technology/edgrants.html

This page features a list with links and descriptions of technology-related grants offered by the U.S. Department of Education.

U.S. Department of Education Funding Opportunities

http://www.ed.gov/topics/topics.jsp?&top=Grants+%26+Contracts

The U.S. DOE's site provides information on finding and applying for government grants. Be sure to read the "What I Should Know About ED Grants" paper that explains everything you need to know before applying.

U.S. Department of Education Grants and Contracts Information

http://www.ed.gov/GrantApps/

Features constantly updated information about grants currently available from the U.S. Department of Education, grant requirements, and application procedures.

World of Knowledge Foundation

http://www.worldofknowledge.org

The World of Knowledge Foundation helps people in America's culturally diverse communities, foreign national students and immigrants by providing funds (through competition) for college.

Writing a Successful Grant Proposal

http://www.mcf.org/mcf/grant/writing.htm

Written by the Minnesota Council on Foundations, this article applies to everyone who has to write grant proposals. Tips are given on writing effective proposals and there is also a question/answer section.

Geography/Environment

50 States and Capitals

http://www.50states.com

An excellent resource if you need to plan a lesson on Michigan or any of the other 49 states. Contains interesting and sometimes humorous information about all the states. Beware the embedded advertisements.

African Wildlife Foundation

http://www.awf.org

From aardvarks to zebras, the AWF presents pages on all kinds of animals for students young and old. Highlights of the site are the sections on the different geographical areas of Africa. There are also stories and reports on conservation efforts spearheaded by the AWF.

Atlapedia Online

http://www.atlapedia.com

Atlapedia Online contains key information on every country of the world. Each country profile provides facts and data on geography, climate, people, religion, language, history, and economy, making it ideal for personal or family education and students of all ages. Another nice section of the site is the Class Resources area, which provides information for students and teachers.

CIA World Fact Book

http://www.cia.gov/cia/publications/factbook/

An incredible free resource for students and teachers (and anyone interested in other countries). From Afghanistan to Zimbabwe, and all countries in between, the CIA presents a wealth of facts at your fingertips.

Climate Ark

http://www.climateark.org

The Climate Ark tracks current environmental issues like climate change and renewable energy, providing links to pertinent articles on the Internet. A great place to keep abreast of the latest environmental treaty or research, this site is best suited for high school students.

Country Studies from the Library of Congress

http://lcWeb2.loc.gov/frd/cs/cshome.html

Part of the Library of Congress Website, 101 different country and area studies are provided with more being added all the time. These are very, very extensive studies with much more than you'll probably need to know, but they are well-designed and easy to navigate.

Dan's Wild Wild Weather Page

http://www.wildwildweather.com

An interactive weather page for kids. Contains information on virtually every type of weather. Good content and easily understood.

Destination: Himalayas – Where Earth Meets Sky

http://library.thinkquest.org/10131/

A beautiful site presented in three different versions (if you have a fast connection, try the Java section). Seemingly everything about the Himalayas is covered, including the geography, native flora and fauna, and information on trekking.

Discovery Channel Expeditions

http://dsc.discovery.com/

It's usually difficult to find good educational websites inspired by television, but this site is a great resource. There are many different expeditions offered, covering topics as diverse as roller coasters, epidemics, and the Montserrat volcano. For some reason, though, the site has made the expeditions hard to find. Use their search engine to search for "online expeditions" and you'll find links to all of them.

Earth and Moon Viewer

http://www.fourmilab.ch/earthview/vplanet.html

This is the online version of those expensive clocks. The Earth and Moon Viewer lets you view the Earth showing the day and night regions (you can then zoom in on the night regions and see the lights of the world). You can also view the Earth from various above various cities, from the Moon, or from a satellite. The Moon can be viewed from various places, too.

Earth Vision

http://www.earthvision.net

This excellent eco-aware site has full-length articles on current environmental issues. It also offers daily news items, a comprehensive calendar of events, and a large collection of links to related sites.

Ecology Communications

http://www.ecology.com

A bio-friendly site, mainly for middle school students and higher, Ecology Communications highlights the Gulf Project, an expedition to the deepest parts of the Gulf of Mexico. The site also contains articles and editorials about environmental issues.

EE-Link Environmental Education on the Internet

http://www.nceet.snre.umich.edu

A project of the National Consortium for Environmental Education and Training, this site contains many classroom resources, including online lessons, a great image gallery, and references to other environmental information.

El Niño Theme Page

http://www.pmel.noaa.gov/toga-tao/el-nino/nino-home-low.html

With everything from global warming to decreased test scores being blamed on El Niño, what is really needed is a website that explains what causes El Niño (and La Niña), what the global effects are, and a lot of scientific data collected from around the world. If you have a fast Internet connection, check out the graphics intensive version here:

http://www.pmel.noaa.gov/tao/elnino/nino-home.html

Environmental News Network

http://www.enn.com

Environmental News Network produces high quality, moderated content (stories, radio broadcasts, etc.) related to environmental and science topics. Stay up-to-date with the latest environmental news. One of the best environmental sites.

Geographia

http://www.geographia.com

Features well-written articles on Africa, Asia, the Caribbean, Europe and Latin America. Reads more like travel brochures than academic text, which is probably a good thing.

Geography Education from National Geographic

http://www.nationalgeographic.com/resources/ngo/education/

Many lesson plans and classroom ideas are included. Also featured are a geography discussion forum, many maps, and information on the geography bee.

Geography World

http://members.aol.com/bowermanb/101.html

This is a very nice large collection of links to geography sites on the Internet. The links are nicely categorized and feature pointers to homework help, games, puzzles, and quizzes.

Geology Link

http://www.geologylink.com

Presented by Houghton Mifflin, this site offers up-to-date geology news, links to virtual field trips, and a virtual classroom. The Geology Glossary is particularly useful.

Glacier

http://www.glacier.rice.edu

Glacier is a great site that shows users what it's like to live and work in the perpetual cold. Featuring picture and real-life accounts of arctic scientists at McMurdo Station in Antartica, the site also offers information on arctic weather, oceans, and ice.

Global Warming Information Page

http://www.globalwarming.org

Is it getting hotter out there? Judging by the information on this site, the answer is a definite "yes." Check out the many articles on current research and news about global warming. The student resources section is a very good first stop when starting research.

Great Lakes Net

http://www.great-lakes.net

Everything you or your students will want to know about the Great Lakes, the largest source of fresh water in the world, is included on this site. It is definitely of more use for the upper grades.

Greatest Places

http://www.greatestplaces.org

Lots of illustrations, film clips, and text about seven places: Amazon, Greenland, Iquazu, Madagascar, Namib, Okavango, and Tibet. Also features a "Question of the Week" and a good Mirage Observer section that explains mirages.

Greenpeace

http://www.greenpeace.org

Greenpeace, the major player in environmental activism, has compiled a resource-rich site full of late-breaking news, in-depth stories, press releases, and an excellent multimedia archive of pictures, movies, and sounds.

How Far Is It?

http://www.indo.com/cgi-bin/dist

This is simple but effective. Enter two places, click Look it up!, and you'll get the distance between the two places in miles, kilometers, and nautical miles, with a link for driving directions (6,606 miles between Chicago and Beijing, but no driving directions!). Beware the embedded advertisements.

Infonation

http://cyberschoolbus.un.org/infonation3/menu/advanced.asp

Infonation allows users to compare and contrast demographic information from all of the world's countries. Users select countries, then select information to compare. An easy-to-read table is then presented. From the United Nations.

Map Machine (National Geographic)

http://www.nationalgeographic.com/resources/ngo/maps/

With excellent maps of the world and of individual countries, this site also offers flags, facts, and profiles of the countries of the world and each U.S. state. There is a link to the online Geography Bee game.

Mapquest

http://www.mapquest.com

At this site are street maps from all over the world and an interactive trip atlas. Tell it where you are starting from and where you want to go, and it will tell you how to get there. The Tripquest section is especially useful.

Mathematics of Cartography

http://math.rice.edu/~lanius/pres/map/

This site combines math and mapmaking in an effective way. Students can learn about the history of cartography as well as engage in some mathematical problems. The website makes god use of other places on the Web.

National Geographic

http://www.nationalgeographic.com

The online home of National Geographic. Click on the Magazines link to get links to the National Geographic Explorer classroom magazine. There is a lot more here than just the magazines—be prepared to spend some time just seeing what's available because this is one of the deepest geographic sites on the web.

National Wildlife Federation

http://www.nwf.org

A very extensive site offers mounds of information on almost every imaginable environmental topic. Resources for teachers include lesson plans and information about environmental workshops. There is also lots of information on current environmental issues, the NWF's publications, and much more.

Natural History and Ecology of Homo Sapiens

http://www.accessexcellence.org/AE/AEPC/WWC/1991/

This site presents 58 lesson plans for teaching human ecology in an interesting fashion and from a unique point of view. The plans are detailed and come with graphics that can be printed out and distributed. Lesson topics include water supply, biomes, evolution, urban green space, etc.

Planet Diary

http://www.planetdiary.com

The Planet Diary chronicles what is going on around the planet. The current phenomena section features information on weather events, geological events, and even toxic waste discoveries. Also features a hyperlinked calendar, archived diaries, background information on the phenomena it tracks, and a good section on measurements.

Savage Earth Online

http://www.pbs.org/wnet/savageearth/

This is the companion website to the PBS series. Beautifully illustrated. Offers information on plate tectonics, earthquakes, volcanoes, and tidal waves. Features animations and an Ask the Experts archive of interesting questions and answers. Most libraries will have copies of the videos.

Scorecard

http://www.scorecard.org

Provided by the Environmental Defense Fund. Contains information on current environmental news. Also offers several discussion forums. Most interesting (and a little scary for people in my zip code) is the feature where you enter your zip code and you get a list of the major polluters in your area.

Seven Wonders of the Ancient World

http://ce.eng.usf.edu/pharos/wonders/

Excellent site on the ancient seven wonders. And in case you forgot, the seven wonders are: 1) The Great Pyramid of Egypt, 2) Babylon's Hanging Gardens, 3) Statue of Zeus at Olympia, 4) Temple of Artemis, 5) Mausoleum at Halicarnassus, 6) Colossus of Rhodes, and 7) Alexandria's Lighthouse.

This Dynamic Earth

http://pubs.usgs.gov/publications/text/dynamic.html

Another good site from the U.S. Geological Survey (who, with NASA, may be the best governmental sources of useful educational information). This website covers Plate Tectonics Theory, the history behind the theory, and how it actually tries to account for plate movement. Very well written.

Understanding Earthquakes

http://www.crustal.ucsb.edu/ics/understanding/

Like the name implies, lots of information about earthquakes. Most interesting are the first-hand accounts from Mark Twain, Jack London, Charles Darwin, and John Muir. Features Java animations, an earthquake quiz, and links to other relevant Internet sites.

United States Global Change Data

http://www.gcdis.usgcrp.gov/

A collection of distributed information systems operated by government agencies involved in global change research, GCDIS provides global change data to scientists and researchers, policy makers, educators, industry, and the public at large.

Virtual Field Trips

http://www.field-guides.com

Field trips without permission slips! At this site you and your class can travel to different parts of the world and experience different natural phenomena. The site also details how its trips dovetail with the national standards in science, social science, and technology.

Volcano World

http://www.volcanoworld.org/

Information on every volcano in the world (at least, it seems like every one). You can view the volcanoes currently erupting and even check out short movies of eruptions. Each volcano is fully described. Also features resources for teachers.

World Wide Web Virtual Library- Geography

http://geography.pinetree.org/

The WWW Virtual Library for Geography isn't as extensive as some of the other libraries but it still has a nice set of links to geography-related sites on the Web.

Yellowstone Geographic

http://www.yellowstonegeographic.com

This is a beautifully presented site that contains a lot of information on Yellowstone and Grand Teton national parks. The site offers articles on the latest news and issues affecting the partks. Probably the best feature is the media gallery that features photos, video clips, and sounds.

Government

See the quick reference guide at the end of this section for more government sites.

Copyright Office

http://lcweb.loc.gov/copyright/

This site provides the information and forms you'll need to seek a copyright. Also features lots of information on copyright law.

Department of Education

http://www.ed.gov

The Home Page for the Department of Education. Includes information on the Secretary's Initiatives. All the federal school information you could ask for.

Environmental Protection Agency

http://www.epa.gov

A very extensive site; contains almost any bit of information you want on the government's efforts to protect the environment. For teachers, there are curriculum guides. For students, there are fact sheets on various environmental aspects.

Fedstats

http://www.fedstats.gov

Maintained by the Federal Interagency Council on Statistical Policy. Provides access to the statistics gathered by more than 70 federal agencies.

First Gov.gov

http://www.firstgov.gov

This is the new and official gateway for all things federal government. Think of it as a Yahoo! for Washington. But there's more—it also serves as a gateway for state government resources, too. By combining everything into one site, they're trying to make resources easier to find. You'll have to be the judge as to whether they've succeeded.

House of Representatives

http://www.house.gov

Provides up-to-the-minute news on House happenings, committee schedules, and links to all of the representatives. Very good educational resources section.

Internal Revenue Service

http://www.irs.gov

File your taxes online or find and download hundreds of tax forms. The IRS site also offers tax information and suggestions on tax preparation.

Library of Congress

http://marvel.loc.gov/

From the biggest library in the world comes perhaps one of the best Websites ever. Search for legislative information, browse exhibits, or use their research search tool to search other Internet sites. Categories: Search Engines, Special Exhibits, News and Events, National Library Service for the Blind and Physically Handicapped.

National Archives and Records Administration
http://www.archives.gov/

An excellent government site features educational resources in the digital classroom. Teachers can use archived records for classroom exercises and can take advantage of online lesson plans.

National Science Foundation

http://www.nsf.gov

Everything you need to know about the NSF. Devoted to fostering science and Engineering Research and Education. Categories: Biology, Geosciences, Math, Physical Sciences, Education, Engineering, Polar Research, Links.

Office of Elementary and Secondary Education Programs
http://www.ed.gov/offices/OESE/

The mission of the Office of Elementary and Secondary Education is to promote academic excellence, enhance educational opportunities and equity for all of America's children and families, and to improve the quality of teaching and learning by providing leadership, technical assistance and financial support.

Office of Postsecondary Education Programs
http://www.ed.gov/offices/OPE/

Offers financial aid information for students as well as information on resources for institutions.

Senate

http://www.senate.gov

Take a virtual tour of the Senate, learn about its history, or read the recent legislation under consideration.

United States Geological Survey

http://info.er.usgs.gov

The USGS website provides a wealth of information on all things geologic (e.g., earthquakes), and some things that aren't (e.g., hurricanes). The best feature may be the Ask a Geologist service that puts you and your students in touch with a geologist to ask questions about mountains, rocks, maps, volcanoes, earthquakes, and more.

White House

http://www.whitehouse.gov/WH/Welcome.html

This very heavily visited site has information on the current and past occupants, news releases, and an excellent virtual library.

Yahoo! State Governments

http://dir.yahoo.com/Government/U_S__Government/State_Government/

There is perhaps no better place for finding state government offices and information than this page. Simply click on the state name and you'll see links to the main state website as well as links to governmental offices.

Federal

The White House
http://www.whitehouse.gov

U.S. Senate
http://www.senate.gov

U.S. House of Representatives
http://www.house.gov

Cabinet Departments

Department of Agriculture
http://www.usda.gov

Department of Commerce
http://www.doc.gov

Department of Defense
http://www.defenselink.mil

Department of Education
http://www.ed.gov

Department of Energy
http://www.doe.gov

Department of Health and
Human Services
http://www.os.dhhs.gov

Department of Housing and
Urban Development
http://www.hud.gov

Department of the Interior
http://www.doi.gov

Department of Justice
http://www.usdoj.gov

Department of Labor
http://www.dol.gov

Department of State
http://www.state.gov

Department of Transportation
http://www.dot.gov

Department of the Treasury
http://www.ustreas.gov

Department of Veterans Affairs
http://www.va.gov

Military

U.S. Air Force
http://www.af.mil

U.S. Army
http://www.army.mil

U.S. Coast Guard
http://www.uscg.mil

U.S. Marine Corps
http://www.usmc.mil

U.S. Navy
http://www.navy.mil

Others

Internal Revenue Service
http://www.irs.gov

National Archives and Records
Administration
http://www.nara.gov

National Oceanic and
Atmospheric Administration
http://www.noaa.gov

National Weather Service
http://www.nws.noaa.gov

State Departments of Education

Alabama
http://www.alsde.edu

Alaska
http://www.educ.state.ak.us

Arizona
http://www.ade.state.az.us

Arkansas
http://arkedu.k12.ar.us

California
http://goldmine.cde.ca.gov

Colorado
http://www.cde.state.co.us

Connecticut
http://www.state.ct.us/sde

Delaware
http://www.doe.state.de.us

District of Columbia
http://www.k12.dc.us

Florida
http://www.firn.edu/doe

Georgia
http://www.doe.k12.ga.us

Hawaii
http://www.k12.hi.us

Idaho
http://www.state.id.us

Illinois
http://www.isbe.state.il.us

Indiana
http://www.doe.state.in.us

Iowa
http://www.state.ia.us/educate

Kansas
http://www.ksbe.state.ks.us

Kentucky
http://www.kde.state.ky.us

Louisiana
http://www.doe.state.la.us

Maine
http://janus.state.me.us/education/homepage.htm

Maryland
http://www.msde.state.md.us

Massachusetts
http://info.doe.mass.edu

Michigan
http://www.mde.state.mi.us

Minnesota
http://www.educ.state.mn.us

Mississippi
http://www.mde.k12.ms.us/

Missouri
http://services.dese.state.mo.us

Government

State Departments of Education *(cont.)*

Montana
http://www.metnet.state.mt.us

Nebraska
http://www.nde.state.ne.us

Nevada
http://www.nsn.k12.nv.us/nvdoe

New Hampshire
http://www.state.nh.us/doe

New Jersey
http://www.state.nj.us/education

New Mexico
http://sde.state.nm.us

New York
http://www.nysed.gov

North Carolina
http://www.dpi.state.nc.us

North Dakota
http://www.dpi.state.nd.us

Ohio
http://www.ode.state.oh.us/

Oklahoma
http://sde.state.ok.us

Oregon
http://www.ode.state.or.us

Pennsylvania
http://www.pde.psu.edu

Rhode Island
http://www.ridoe.net/

South Carolina
http://www.sde.state.sc.us

South Dakota
http://www.state.sd.us/state/executive/deca

Tennessee
http://www.state.tn.us/education

Texas
http://www.tea.state.tx.us

Utah
http://www.usoe.k12.ut.us

Vermont
http://www.state.vt.us/educ

Virginia
http://www.pen.k12.va.us

Washington
http://www.k12.wa.us

West Virginia
http://wvde.state.wv.us

Wisconsin
http://www.dpi.state.wi.us

Wyoming
http://www.k12.wy.us

History and Social Studies

1492: An Ongoing Voyage

http://sunsite.unc.edu/expo/1492.exhibit/Intro.html

From the Library of Congress, this site is a feature-packed enriching lesson on the voyage of Columbus and the impacts of the discovery of the New World. It offers maps and other historical documents. Follow the Expo Bus link to see additional sites on the Vatican, the Soviet Union, the Dead Sea Scrolls, and Paleontology.

Academy of Achievement

http://www.achievement.org

A wonderful resource and a very extensive site, the Academy of Achievement extols the achievements of twentieth-century Americans. Each profile includes a short interview while many have audio and video supplements.

American Civil War Homepage

http://sunsite.utk.edu/civil-war/warweb.html

This website serves as a repository for civil war links. The links are divided into various categories. The list is well-maintained and exhaustive in its scope of resources. The site deserves to be called the Civil War Homepage.

American Memory

http://rs6.loc.gov/amhome.html

A very extensive site from the Library of Congress. The historical collections consist of primary documents, photographs, sound clips and more. You'll need to use the Collection Finder to see for yourself just how many resources there are (and there are a lot!).

America's West

http://www.americanwest.com

America's West is a very extensive website that explores the history of the American West and the people and places that made it famous. The site consists mainly of links to other websites.

Ancient Olympics

http://www.perseus.tufts.edu/Olympics

From the Perseus Project, this site details the history of the Olympic Games, offers graphics and information on the ancient sites where the games were held, stories of famous ancient Olympic athletes, and more.

Atlapedia Online

http://www.atlapedia.com

Atlapedia Online contains key information on every country of the world. Each country profile provides facts and data on geography, climate, people, religion, language, history and economy, making it ideal for personal or family education and students of all ages.

Biography of America

http://www.learner.org/biographyofamerica/

Not much you can say about this site but, "Wow!" The companion site to the video series covers American history from the first new world encounters to the present day. With intelligent text, wonderful maps and images, and transcripts from the videos, this is one of the best sites on the web.

Colonial Williamsburg

http://www.history.org

The Almanac section of the Colonial Williamsburg Foundation's website provides extensive information on Colonial Williamsburg, including its history, buildings, and people.

Core Documents of U.S. Democracy

http://www.access.gpo.gov/su_docs/dpos/coredocs.html

They're all here, from the Bill of Rights to the Declaration of Independence, complete and with narrative text explaining their importance and nuances. Categories: Legislative and Legal, Regulatory, Office of the President, Demographic, Economic, and Miscellaneous.

AEA 267 Social Studies Sites

http://www.aea267.k12.ia.us/curriculum/socialstudies.html

Presented by AEA 267, one of twelve area education agencies of Iowa, this page contains a list of Social Studies sites on the Web in more than 15 categories. This is a good place to start looking for Internet information on such topics as American History or Government.

Discoverers Web

http://www.win.tue.nl/cs/fm/engels/discovery

If you are looking for resources on discoverers, issues about the discovery of new places, and information on anything else pertaining to discovery, this site will suffice. No original content, but a very good list of links (in chronological order) that point to the Web's vast resources on the topic.

Egyptology

http://www.egyptology.com

Egyptology.com explores the art, archaeology, religion and history of Egypt. The site offers an inside view of the tomb of Niankhkhnum and Khnumhotep, a gallery of paintings and pictures, and more.

Exploring Ancient World Cultures

http://eawc.evansville.edu/

This is a great resource (though a little text-heavy). It contains information, primary texts, and more on the ancient cultures of the Near East, India, Egypt, China, Greece, Rome, Islam and Europe.

Eyewitness—History Through the Eyes of Those Who Lived It

http://www.ibiscom.com

Using diaries, interviews, newspaper stories, and other first-hand sources, this site recounts historical events such as Custer's Last Stand and the Great San Francisco Earthquake.

Famous Trials

http://www.law.umkc.edu/faculty/projects/ftrials/ftrials.htm

This site provides detailed information on some of the most famous trials in American and World history, including the Scopes "Monkey" Trial, the Amistad Trials, the trial of Socrates and the Salem Witchcraft Trials.

Flints and Stones—Life in Prehistory

http://museums.ncl.ac.uk/flint/menu.html

An excellent site that takes you on a tour of life in prehistoric times. It blows away the myths and legends surrounding prehistory and manages to be educational and interesting at the same time. No Fred or Wilma here!

Histor eSearch

http://www.snowcrest.net/jmike

Excellent categorical listing of history resources on the Internet. Sites have been previewed for quality of academic content. The design of the site detracts a little from its usefulness but it is still filled with many quality resources.

Historical Atlas of the 20th Century

http://www.erols.com/mwhite28/20centry.htm

With easy-to-read maps, this Atlas vividly shows trends in government, living conditions, population, and other demographic trends in the world of the 20th century.

Historical Text Archive

http://historicaltextarchive.com/

Here's some good reading. This site provides historical texts from the United States and other countries. There's more here than just dry proclamations and laws. The site includes diaries and personal accounts from people involved in the historical event.

History Buff's Home Page

http://www.historybuff.com

History Buff looks at history from the point of view of the fourth estate. The press coverage from major, and not-so-major, events is depicted in replications of newspaper articles, audio recordings, etc.

History Channel

http://www.historychannel.com

This excellent site features special history events. Check out the Real Audio collection of historic sound clips and speeches. Also, don't miss This Day in History, which lets you search for the events that happened on any day of the year.

History Net

http://www.thehistorynet.com

The History Net is a valuable resource for those interested in history. This website collects articles from more than 15 magazines (American History, British Heritage, Historic Traveler, etc.) and posts the full-text articles. Unfortunately, the site has been combined with About.com so you'll notice the pop-up windows and a lot of advertising.

History Place

http://www.historyplace.com

Nicely illustrated site. Features an eclectic mix of exhibits, including major speeches of Abraham Lincoln, the child labor investigative photos of Lewis W. Hine, and a photo history of John F. Kennedy. Also offers a photo and a speech of the week.

History/Social Studies for K–12 Teachers

http://www.execpc.com/~dboals/boals.html

Probably the biggest repository of links to social studies sites on the web, this great resource is updated daily with the latest websites. The sites are logically categorized and easy to browse.

History's Best on PBS

http://www.pbs.org/history

This is PBS's companion site to their history programs. The websites are, for the most part, as educational and as well produced as the PBS shows that inspired them.

HyperHistory

http://www.hyperhistory.com/online_n2/History_n2/a.html

This site contains time lines with links to stories on major world events. Based on the synchronoptic (clickable time line with text and images) concept, it functions as a companion to the seminal World History Chart—a very effective resource for all students and teachers.

Hypertext on American History

http://odur.let.rug.nl/~usa/usa.htm

Featuring a complete text on American History, this site also provides many other resources, chief among them are historical documents and speeches. This is also one of the few websites that has almost every State of the Nation and Inauguration speech from all of the presidents.

Inventor of the Week

http://web.mit.edu/afs/athena.mit.edu/org/i/invent/i-main.html

If you need information on inventors (like Philo Farnsworth) and inventions (Philo invented television), this is the place to see. The archives list inventors and inventions alphabetically, and offer images and descriptive text on each entry.

Kings and Queens of Europe

http://www.camelotintl.com/royal/europe.html

For those of use who cannot tell one king or queen from the other, this site comes to the rescue. The rulers are catalogued by time period and country, with each entry providing a description and a hyperlinked family history.

Matewan

http://www.matewan.com

One of the most famous small towns in America, Matewan was the site of bloody coal mine wars and wars of another kind (the infamous Hatfield and McCoy feud). The town proves proud of its history by providing information about both, as well as links for more information.

National Archives Online Exhibit Hall

http://www.archives.gov/exhibit_hall/

The Exhibit Hall features information on history in documents (Japanese surrender), history in pictures (panoramic photographs), and history as surreal (Elvis meeting Nixon). This is a very good site that uses primary sources to document American history.

National History Day

http://www.nationalhistoryday.org/

Home page of National History Day, a program promoting the study of history in school. Though called History "Day," it is really a year-long project. A teacher's guide is available on the site to give guidance on how to incorporate this program into your teaching.

Our Timelines.com

http://www.ourtimelines.com/

This is a very cool site. Enter your year of birth and an ending date and a time line is created showing many of the major events that have occurred during your lifetime. It even tells you how old you were when the event happened.

Perseus Project

http://www.perseus.tufts.edu

The Perseus Project is an ever-growing digital library devoted to the study of the ancient world. This website is very comprehensive and features long articles, maps of the ancient world, text tools, encyclopedias and much more.

Pop History Now!

http://www.pophistorynow.com/

If you need some popular culture information, this site tries to please. Each day it features a different week in American pop culture from the 1940s to the 1990s, with news items, entertainment tidbits, and more. Free membership registration is required to access some of the site.

Slave Voices

http://odyssey.lib.duke.edu/slavery

From the Special Collections Library of Duke University. The story of slavery is retold with the documents of the period, including bills of sale, newspaper advertisements, diaries, etc., which are reproduced and interpreted.

Social Studies Lesson Plans and Resources

http://www.csun.edu/~hcedu013

Over 100 social studies lesson plans are provided by Dr. Marty Levine, Professor of Secondary Education, California State University, Northridge (CSUN). It is a very good set of resources. There is also information on teaching strategies, online activities, and related newsgroups and mailing lists.

Social Studies Projects

http://www.eduplace.com/projects/ssproj.html

This site serves as an exchange for educators to collaborate on many online social studies projects. Includes lesson plans and ideas on weather, geography, and more.

Teacher's Guide to the Holocaust

http://fcit.coedu.usf.edu/holocaust

This is a well-designed, very informative, and sobering site that presents the history of the Holocaust, its immediate and long-term effects, and much more. The website also offers a useful Teacher Resources section.

This Day in History (from the History Channel)

http://www.historychannel.com/tdih

This is probably the best "This Day" site on the web. Each day one event is featured (often with an accompanying video or audio clip). Other events are also listed, as well as links to This Day in Wall Street, Automotive, and Civil War History.

Titanic-The Unsinkable Ship and Halifax, Nova Scotia

http://titanic.gov.ns.ca

A lot of information on the Titanic. You can view artifacts, read the wireless transcript excerpt, and even view the list of Titanic victims buried in Halifax.

U.S. Historical Documents

http://www.law.ou.edu/hist

From the Magna Carta to the 2002 State of the Union Address and everything in between, this site has the historical record of the United States in hypertext format. Very nice!

Words and Deeds in American History

http://lcweb2.loc.gov/ammem/mcchtml/corhome.html

From the Library of Congress. A huge collection of documents that illustrate the history of American government, politics, and culture.

World of Benjamin Franklin

http://sln.fi.edu/franklin/rotten.html

A "virtual" book on Benjamin Franklin, it is included in this guide not so much because of its content, which is outstanding, but because it serves as an example of what a class can post on the Web as a group. The site also contains a video clip and even some electrical safety tips.

Primary Sources and Activities for the Classroom— U.S. National Archives & Records Administration (NARA)

http://www.archives.gov/digital_classroom/index.html

A social studies teacher's dream! A wonderful site for finding primary sources and lessons to go with them. For a special treat for you and your students, check out the online exhibits at the Exhibit Hall.

World Wide Web Virtual Library-History

http://www.ku.edu/history/VL/

This website is an incredibly large collection of links to other history sites on the Web. There are more than 100 subcategories alone, and the list of links is many times the number of categories.

Language Arts

Alphabet Superhighway

http://www.ash.udel.edu/ash/

The Alphabet Superhighway offers teachers the opportunity to let their classes create and post Cyberzines, classroom portfolios, website projects, and much more. The ASH offers a discussion forum for teachers to share ideas and data with others around the world.

Aphorism's Galore

http://www.ag.wastholm.net/

If you're looking for a short, witty quote, Aphorism's Galore could have just what you need. Their database features thousands of aphorisms by famous authors, artists, and the ever-popular "anonymous."

Art of Storytelling

http://www.eldrbarry.net/roos/art.htm

Perhaps the best storytelling website of them all. This site features a manual for beginners, Effective Storytelling, as well a list of storytelling book recommendations, and many links to other storytelling sites.

Authors and Illustrators

http://www.dalton.org/libraries/fairrosa/cl.authors.html

This page has links to hundreds of websites devoted to an author, an illustrator, or their work.

Banned Books

http://www.ala.org/bbooks

Part of the American Library Association's site, this page includes information about how books are banned, the most challenged and banned books, and the most challenged and banned authors in the U.S. for the last year.

Booklist

http://www.ala.org/booklist/

From the American Library Association, the online companion to the Booklist magazine. The site offers current reviews on books for youth, as well as reviews of media, reference materials, and books for adults.

Bulwer-Lytton Fiction Contest

http://www.bulwer-lytton.com

The site where WWW means Wretched Writers Welcome. Sponsored by the English Department at San Jose State University, the trick is to compose the opening sentence to the worst of all possible novels (for example, "it was a dark and stormy night"). Read the past winners' entries to see what never to do.

Carol Hurst's Children's Literature Site

http://www.carolhurst.com

This site is one of the best in this category. It offers many resources about children's literature, not the least of these being lesson plans in U.S. history, geography, reading, writing, and science

Children's Literature Activities for the Classroom

http://www.marcias-lesson-links.com/ChildrensLit.html

Hundreds of literature activities, organized by grade level (preschool through grade 6) and genre (American historical, Women's History, Fairy Tales, Mythology, and others). There are also links to children's authors and booklists.

Children's Literature Web Guide

http://www.ucalgary.ca/~dkbrown

This is one of the best websites there is. There are more resources to literacy and children's reading than just about anywhere else. You'll also find a comprehensive list of book award winners, teaching ideas, and a great collection of annotated links.

Cool Word of the Day

http://www.edu.yorku.ca/wotd

If you or your students want to enrich their vocabulary, this is a good daily stop. This site has, as the title says, a "cool" word of the day, with definition, and also accepts submissions.

Create Your Own Newspaper

http://crayon.net

A free site, CRAYON lets its 300,000 subscribers, kids and adults, create their very own newspaper. With downloadable links to real newspaper and broadcast stories and graphics, this is a great place to experiment and learn the ins and outs of journalism.

Encyclopedia Mythica

http://pantheon.org/mythica

The definitive online encyclopedia on mythology, folklore, and legend. The encyclopedia contains more than 5,300 entries, some full-length while others are just term definitions.

Fabulous Fiction

http://www.fabfiction.com

A great site to visit as a class. An introductory paragraph is posted online and someone else takes up the story from there, but only writing a paragraph or so before handing it off to someone else. This is a good example of using the web for collaboration among writers and students.

Grammar Bytes

http://www.chompchomp.com

This interactive grammar review offers an index of grammar terms, interactive exercises, and a short list of grammar rules with explanations. Probably more suited for the younger author.

Grammar Lady

http://www.grammarlady.com

The grammar lady answers grammar questions and posts online articles about grammar use (and misuse). There is also a free hotline service which you can call and ask your grammar question.

Grandpa Tucker's Rhymes and Tales

http://www.night.net/tucker

This website is full of amusing tales, stories, songs, and rhymes. The Poetry Pencil is particularly worthwhile, consisting of poems submitted by children.

KidBibs

http://www.kidbibs.com

KidBibs is a teaching and parenting resource site designed to support children's reading, writing, and learning. The website offers articles on the language arts written by respected researchers as well as other information on how you can encourage reading and writing.

KidsRead.com

http://www.kidsreads.com

This is a wonderful site for the avid young reader. KidsRead offers information on kids' favorite books, series, and authors. The site is well-designed and information is easy to find. There are also games, book reviews, and contests.

Literary Resources on the Net

http://www.andromeda.rutgers.edu/~jlynch/Lit/

Almost anything you want to find about literacy is categorized (e.g., Renaissance, American, Theatre and Drama, Women's Literature, etc.)—a good place to start your research.

Literature and Language—Sites for Children

http://www.ala.org/parentspage/greatsites/lit.html

Compiled by a division of the American Library Association, this site has links to hundreds of literature and languages sites (some of them are commercial sites, though). There are also sections with links to science and technology as well as arts and entertainment sites.

National Right to Read Foundation

http://www.nrrf.org/

If you're looking for information on the usefulness of phonics, the NRRF's site is a place to visit. A vocal proponent of phonics, the foundation offers information on phonics as well as news about Reading First. The partisanship of the organization shows in their online satires.

National Storytelling Festival

http://www.storytellingfestival.net/

Presented by ITV.net, this website has audio and video clips of storytelling from the recent festival. Also available are tips on storytelling from storytellers.

Online Books Page

http://digital.library.upenn.edu/books/

One of the hidden treasures of the web. This site is a categorical list of more than 17,000 online texts. A highlight of the site is the Features section, which features resources on such topics as women writers, banned books, and literature prize winners.

Online English Grammar

http://www.edufind.com/english/grammar

A great online grammar book, it is searchable alphabetically or by topic. Also featured are sound files for pronunciation rules.

Phonics Room

http://members.aol.com/phonicsrm

If you haven't totally been swept away by the whole language movement, you still may need some phonics activities. This site has many activities organized by the letters of the alphabet (though not all letters are represented).

Poetry Archives

http://www.emule.com/poetry

The Poetry Archives features classical poetry from hundreds of authors, from Bronte to Bronte, Keats to Yeats. The site also offers a discussion board and a mailing list that will send you poetry via e-mail.

Poetry on KidzPage

http://www.veeceet.com/

An excellent poetry site. You'll find an eclectic mix of poems, ranging from Jabberwocky and poems by Ogden Nash to many pages of student submitted poems. Poetry submission guidelines are available on the site.

Poetry Resource

http://www.pmpoetry.com

The Poetry resource is a great collection of links to other poetry sites. Categories include Poets, Poems, Poetry Around the World, Poetry through Time, Organizations, Publishers, and more.

Project Gutenberg

http://promo.net/pg

Online books, lots of them, and online short stories, online government documents, and online many things in print. Project Gutenberg was originally conceived as a computer repository of printed material, and their database keeps growing and growing. This site is one of the reasons the Internet thrives.

Reading First

http://www.nclb.gov/parents/

Part of the No Child Left Behind Act, Reading First is the latest governmental effort to reform education. This site offers some good resources for parents on how to help their children with reading and homework. It's part of the larger No Child Left Behind site, located here: http://www.nclb.gov

Stories and Fairy Tales Theme Page

http://www.cln.org/themes/fairytales.html

Offering links to other sites, this page is a meta-list of stories, folklore, and fairy tale themes from around the world. You'll find Christmas stories, tall tales, lesson plan ideas and much more.

TeenLit.com

http://www.teenlit.com

The purpose of TeenLit.com is to promote Teen Literacy by providing a forum for teen writers to publish and discuss their writing, review and discuss books they read, and to provide a resource for their teachers. The site is administered by two Michigan teachers.

Vocabulary.com

http://www.vocabulary.com

For anyone interested in increasing their vocabulary, Vocabulary University offers puzzles and other special features. Designed for students from upper-elementary to college. There are also printable puzzles, thematic ideas, and a lot more. Definitely worth a visit.

Wordsmyth

http://www.wordsmyth.net

What separates this online dictionary and thesaurus from the others is that it integrates with your browser. Once you have put a special page from the site on your browser's toolbar, you can highlight a word on a web page, click on the Wordsmyth button on your browser, and a new page will open giving you the definition of the highlighted word. Wordsmyth also offers a lively discussion board focused on either general issues or a question of the month.

Lesson Plans

Academy Curriculum Exchange

http://ofcn.org/cyber.serv/academy/ace/

A collection of lesson plans in the areas of Language Arts, mathematics, Social Studies, Science and miscellaneous. Plans are divided by grade level, and include elementary through high school grades.

Arithmetic Lesson Plans

http://mathforum.org/arithmetic/arith.units.html

This page lists what the site creator calls the "best" lesson plans. And they are very good. The page is made more valuable by the good link descriptions included. There are also more plans available in the Mathematics Library.

AskERIC Lesson Plans

http://askeric.org/Virtual/Lessons/

AskERIC offers more than 2,000 lesson plans submitted by practicing teachers in these general categories: Arts, Educational Technology, Foreign Language, Health, Interdisciplinary, Language Arts, Mathematics, Physical Education, Science, Social Studies, and Vocational Education.

Awesome Library

http://www.awesomelibrary.org/

Featuring more than 22,000 links, each main category in the Awesome Library collection has a section on lesson plans, and each lesson plans section contains many links to lesson plans on the web. Be sure to check out the other sections— they may not be lesson plans, but there are a lot of good teacher resources in there.

Blue Web'N Learning Sites Library

http://www.kn.pacbell.com/wired/bluewebn

A searchable database of tutorials, activities, lesson plans, etc. Very useful and well organized. Categories: Art, Business, English, Foreign Language, Health and Physical Education, History and Social Studies, Math, Science, Technology, and more.

Curriculum Archive

http://www.buildingrainbows.com/CA/ca.home.php

This website is a great resource for teachers. Lesson plans are organized first by grade (preschool-undergraduate) and then by subject. Users of the plans then submit comments. Teachers who submit lessons can be paid for them.

Columbia Education Center Lesson Plans

http://www.col-ed.org/cur

An easily navigable site featuring hundreds of lesson plans for K-12 teachers, submitted by other teachers. The plans are categorized by subject and grade level.

Community Learning Network Themes

http://www.cln.org/themes_index.html

This is one of the best sites in this section. The CLN has compiled curricular and instructional material links on a myriad of topics. The website makes for easy navigation and you're sure to find something here to use.

Core Knowledge - Lesson Plans

http://www.coreknowledge.org/CKproto2/resrcs/

Another good collection of lesson plans, these were submitted by practicing teachers. Plans are for classrooms up to and including grade 8, and are organized by grade level and subject.

Discovery Channel School

http://school.discovery.com/teachers/

Excellent site for teachers. A database of lesson plans and resources, organized by grade. Many online activities covering the many different topics of science, from cloning to archaeology. Be sure to check out the puzzle collection.

Lesson Plans – Microsoft Education

http://www.microsoft.com/education/LessonPlans.aspx

Here you will find a searchable database of lessons that incorporate the use of technology. The lessons span kindergarten through college and virtually every subject area. You can also search for lessons written for specific Microsoft products.

Gateway to Educational Materials

http://www.thegateway.org

The GEM is a searchable database of links to other collections of educational materials on the web. It is searchable by keyword, grade, and subject.

Hands-On Technology Program

http://www.galaxy.net/~k12/

A collection of activities with each one including a list of needed materials, step-by-step instructions, and teacher notes. The categories are Physical Science, Life Science, Earth Science, and Math for grades 1-6.

Houghton Mifflin Activity Search

http://www.eduplace.com/search/activity.html

Search by grade level and activity: Language Arts, Math, Social Studies, Science, and Art. You can also browse by theme.

Learning Web

http://www.usgs.gov/education

This is the educational resources portion of the U.S. Geological Survey's website. There are many lessons available, including Working with Maps, Earth Hazards, and Global Change.

Learning with Mysteries

http://www.mysterynet.com/learn

Hundreds of lesson plans and ideas for using online mysteries in the classroom. Features current and archived mysteries that incorporate reading, writing, spelling and art skills.

Lessons Plans 4 Teachers

http://www.lessonplans4teachers.com/

This site will link you to the Web's top rated lessons in just about every subject. You will also find links for help with lesson planning and finding lessons. Also useful are the rubrics, grade book software suggestions, and information about online education degrees.

Lessons Plans Page

http://www.lessonplanspage.com/

More than 1,500 lesson plans, nicely arranged by grade (preschool to 12th) and subject. This site has also recently added a lively discussion site and a new feature called American Teachers, with even more resources for teachers.

LessonPlanz.com

http://www.lessonplanz.com/

A huge site aiming to be the resource for online lesson plans. This site currently links to thousands of lesson plans pages, all hand-picked and reviewed by the author of the site. The plans are logically categorized and easy to find. A very good site.

Math Lesson Plans

http://askeric.org/Virtual/Lessons/

Many math lesson plans (text only) applicable to mostly grades K-8. Categories include algebra, applied math, arithmetic, functions, geometry, measurement, probability, process skills, and statistics.

Music Education Launch Site

http://www.talentz.com/MusicEducation/

The Music Education Launch Site features lessons plans for teachers of elementary, middle school, and high school students. It also has plans for the teachers of band, orchestra, and voice.

NASA - Education Program

http://education.nasa.gov

Very good resource provided by NASA. Lesson plans on remote sensing, biodiversity, and understanding light. They also provide tips on how to interact with NASA to use their missions as part of your classroom activities. There's a lot here besides lesson plans and the site is definitely worth a look.

Natural History and Ecology of Homo Sapiens

http://www.accessexcellence.org/AE/AEPC/WWC/1991/

This site presents many lesson plans for teaching human ecology in an interesting fashion and from a unique point of view. The plans are detailed and come with graphics that can be printed out and distributed. Lesson topics include water supply, biomes, evolution, urban green space, etc.

New York Times Learning Network

http://www.nytimes.com/learning

Tons of resources for teachers. Geared more for high school students. Daily and archived lesson plans in 15 categories. The plans are detailed and often include references to National Content Standards. This is an excellent education resource.

NOVA Online | Teachers

http://www.pbs.org/wgbh/nova/teachers/

The popular PBS science program offers lesson resources for each of its broadcasts. There are suggested activities before and after watching the program, as well as activity sheets and more.

Printable Worksheets

http://www.kidsdomain.com/grown/links/Printable_Worksheets.html

If you need some seatwork material, then make sure to visit this website. They offer a collection of many different sheets and links to other sites offering similar materials.

Science Lessons

http://www.reachoutmichigan.org/funexperiments/agesubject/subject.html

If you're looking for science lesson plans, check out Reach Out Michigan. They offer a collection of lesson plans in the areas of astronomy, biology, chemistry, earth science, physical science, and technology. Plans are for early elementary through high school.

SeaWorld Educational Resources

http://www.seaworld.org/teacherguides

SeaWorld provides lesson plans and teacher's guide for a variety of subjects, all relating to life in and around the ocean, of course.

Social Studies Lesson Plans and Resources

http://www.csun.edu/~hcedu013

Over 100 social studies lesson plans, provided by Dr. Marty Levine, Professor of Secondary Education, California State University, Northridge. A very good set of resources. Categories: Lesson Plans and Teaching Strategies, Online Activities, Teaching Current Events.

Teacher Talk Forum-Lesson Plans

http://education.indiana.edu/cas/ttforum/lesson.html

One page that offers links to lesson plans in 20 different categories, including home economics, icebreakers, reasoning, and conflict resolution.

Teaching Ideas for Primary Teachers

http://www.teachingideas.co.uk

An excellent site from the U.K. Teachers have submitted their ideas for teaching various subjects in twelve areas. These aren't strictly "lesson plans," but they can be used in addition to your planned activities.

Teachnet.com

http://www.teachnet.com

Many lesson plans are provided by teachers in a variety of categories: art, health-physical education, Internet, music, language, math, science, social studies, and miscellaneous.

Theme-Related Resources on the World Wide Web

http://www.stemnet.nf.ca/CITE/themes.html

This website offers more than thirty different theme categories. Each theme is a collection of example work or links to relevant websites. This is a great teacher resource.

Topic Enrichment from World Book

http://www2.worldbook.com/educators/lesson_plans_index.asp

World Book has collected many resources you can use to supplement your lessons. Each topic list here includes excerpts and graphics from the encyclopedia, as well as suggested classroom activities and reading lists. There are plans for preschool, and the subject areas of English, Science, Social Studies, and Math are covered, too.

Trash to Treasures

http://craftsforkids.about.com/library/bltrashtr.htm?once=true&

This is a big list of items you can use in your arts and crafts lessons. Each item has many different activities, and full instructions are included. This is just one section of the larger About.com crafts section.

Weather Unit

http://faldo.atmos.uiuc.edu/WEATHER/weather.html

You've probably heard of "writing across the curriculum." This site provides "weather across the curriculum." It is, in short, a weather unit that is integrated into Math, Science, Language Arts, Social Studies, Geography, Art, Music, Drama, and Physical Education. Be sure to check out the link to the Curriculum Archive which hosts another large set of lesson resources.

Mathematics

21st Century Problem Solving

http://www2.hawaii.edu/suremath/home.html

Focused on problem solving, this site is dedicated to helping students learn how to solve word problems. Includes valuable teacher materials and areas in Math, Physics, and Chemistry.

A+Math

http://www.aplusmath.com

Offers interactive features like flashcards, puzzles, and games. The Homework Helper lets students enter their math problems (addition, subtraction, multiplication, and division) and their answers and get immediate feedback (but they won't get the right answer!).

Algebra Story and Word Problems

http://www2.hawaii.edu/suremath/intro_algebra.html

This site focuses on the process of problem solving as it pertains to Algebra. Scroll down the homepage to see the "meat" of the website. Amidst the useful problem-solving advice are links to other good algebra-related sites.

American Mathematical Society—eMath

http://e-math.ams.org

The online home of the American Mathematical Society, this site offers information about the society, links to useful math-related places on the Web, and organization information.

Appetizers and Lessons for Math and Reason

http://whyslopes.com

This useful site features activities that teachers can use to introduce a mathematical concept or to fill up those last five minutes of the lesson when everything else has been done. Many fine activities here. Students will also find advice on how to study math.

Ask Dr. Math

http://mathforum.org/dr.math/

This very good site answers math questions you send in. The questions and answers are archived for searching, and divided among elementary/middle school and high school/college/and beyond. All of the questions and answers are archived.

Beat the Calculator

http://mathforum.org/k12/mathtips/beatcalc.html

From the BEATCALC mailing list. An archive of more than 160 tips to solving mathematical problems quickly (quicker than a calculator?). Includes tips on squaring, multiplying, dividing, adding, subtracting and finding percents.

Brain Teasers

http://www.eduplace.com/math/brain

Divided among grades 3–4, 5–6, and 7–8, these brainteasers can be used for lesson openers or to integrate math into other parts of the curriculum. One teaser is presented each week, though archived teasers are available.

Education 4 Kids

http://www.edu4kids.com

Features online flash cards, a math square game, and drills for math tables, time, and money. Fast loading for questions and answers.

Everyday Mathematics

http://www.kent.wednet.edu/curriculum/math/edmath/

The Everyday Mathematics Resource Guide offers resources for teachers in grades K-6. The site contains lesson plans, ideas shared by teachers, and lists of links to related websites.

Exploratorium

http://www.exploratorium.edu/explore/handson.html

This site is bursting with interesting hands-on science and math activities. Each activity is well-presented with diagrams, materials lists, online tutorials, background information, and additional links to peruse. A truly wonderful resource for the math or science teacher.

Flashcards for Kids

http://www.edu4kids.com/math/

Flashcards for Kids lets users select the type of math (addition, subtraction, etc.), the complexity of the problems, and the number of digits. It then presents a series of flashcard problems and gives quick feedback on the answers.

Fun Mathematics Lessons

http://math.rice.edu/~lanius/Lessons

Well-organized lessons from Cynthia Lanius that are designed to make math fun for students. Includes lessons on geometry, transformations, and more.

Fun With Numbers

http://newdream.net/~sage/old/numbers/

A good resource in its own way, this site features many things that you would not want to figure out on your own, including the first 28,915 odd primes, the first 999 factorials, and 1.2 million digits of pi.

Geometry Center

http://www.scienceu.com/geometry

The Geometry Center offers lots of information on geometry presented with colorful graphics. Featured is information on triangle tilings and polyhedra, symmetry and tiling, and tetrahedral puzzles.

Gordon's Games

http://www3.telus.net/public/m.games/welcome.html

Gordon's Games offers hundreds of mathematical challenges for students in K-3. You can print these pages out or purchase the booklets at cost..

History of Mathematics

http://turnbull.dcs.st-and.ac.uk/~history/

Extensive resources on the history of mathematics. Includes hundreds of biographies of famous mathematicians, quotes (with a search engine), and comprehensive lists of math award winners. The best math history site on the Web.

Interactive Mathematics Online

http://tqd.advanced.org/2647

This is a very detailed and informative site that presents information on Algebra, Chaos, Geometry, and Trigonometry. There is also a section that lets you create your own Stereograms and some useful Java applets.

Lemonade Stand

http://www.coolmath4kids.com/lemonade

Teach math and such economic concepts as supply and demand by letting your students run a virtual lemonade stand. Student have to set a price, determine quantity, and decide how much to spend on advertising (while not inflating their earnings!). It's a very good site, though it does carry advertisements (which is an economics lesson in itself, I guess).

Math Archives - Topics in Mathematics

http://archives.math.utk.edu

THE math resource site on the Web. Hundreds of links (fully searchable) in forty different categories ranging from Algebra to Partial Differential Equations (which is apparently some kind of math).

Math Goodies

http://www.mathgoodies.com

Math Goodies features interactive math lessons with a problem-solving approach. In addition to the many lessons, the website features math chat rooms, homework help, and online calculators.

Math Reference

http://www.math2.org/

Featured are many math tables and tips on using them (check out the tip for remembering multiplying 9s!). But the site is a lot more than just math tables—it acts more like a portal to other math-related sites on the web.

MathCounts

http://mathcounts.org

MathCounts is a national coaching and competition program for 7th and 8th grade students. This website offers information on the program as well as math problems of the week.

Mathematics

http://galaxy.einet.net/galaxy/Science/Mathematics.html

This search-engine-like site offers hundreds of links to math resources in many categories, which includes academic organizations, articles, collections, directories, discussion groups, periodicals, and more.

MathMol K-12 Activity Page

http://www.nyu.edu/pages/mathmol/K_12.html

MathMol presents Mathematics and Molecules. There are hypermedia textbooks for grades 3–5 and 6–12, a water module for K–12 students, and much more.

Mega-Mathematics

http://wwwc3.lanl.gov/mega-math/

Bringing "unusual and important mathematical ideas to elementary school classrooms," this site presents math in a creative and understandable way. Each section offers activities, vocabulary, and information on big ideas and concepts.

Mint

http://www.themint.org

This site does a lot to answer the question as to whether math is important in everyday life. Students can start their own businesses, learn how to be millionaires by saving and investing, and learn about government spending, all while using math.

Plane Math

http://www.planemath.com

This is a good site that teaches mathematics through aeronautics to students with physical disabilities. Students research, design, plot courses, do air traffic control, and more. Teachers can register their classes to be eligible for prizes.

Professor Freeman's Math Help

http://www.mathpower.com

There's just as much help for teachers here as there is for students. Professor Freedman offers tips to reduce math anxiety, suggestions to improve study skills, and information about learning styles.

S.O.S. Math

http://www.sosmath.com

Designed more for students in high school and college, this website provides tons of information on Algebra, Trigonometry, Calculus, Matrix Algebra, Complex Variables, and Differential Equations (which, I'm assuming, is some kind of math thing). Excellent site.

Word Problems for Kids

http://www.stfx.ca/special/mathproblems/welcome.html

If a car left Detroit and traveled sixty miles an hour for nine hours… You get the idea. From Canada, a very good site devoted to math word problems for grades 5–12.

World Wide Web Virtual Library - Math

http://euclid.math.fsu.edu/Science/math.html

This Virtual Library offers a wealth of resources, including links to electronic math journals, math newsgroups, and links to other math sites on the Web.

Multimedia

Many of these sites require a browser plug-in or other multimedia software program. Listed below are the most popular plug-ins, and links to where you can download them. All are free and each is available for both Windows and Mac platforms. Each site has listed the required plug-in. If the site would require a fast connection to view it properly, that is noted as well. It is recommend that you periodically visit the download sites for updates to your software.

Adobe Acrobat PDF

http://www.adobe.com/prodindex/acrobat/readstep.html

The Adobe Acrobat viewer, available free from Adobe, allows you to view documents in the PDF format. This format is used by some web developers because the formatting of the document is faithfully retained. That is, the PDF document looks just like the printed copy. This is preferable over the HTML format that is used to write web pages since HTML cannot preserve original formatting.

Flash

http://www.macromedia.com

The Flash player is a plug-in for your browser. With it, you can view some of the most dynamic and visually appealing sites on the web. Flash allows web designers to incorporate movement, sound, and interaction in ways that are impossible with standard HTML. The Macromedia site also has links to some of the most innovative Flash sites, which are well worth visiting even if some are just eye candy.

RealAudio

http://www.real.com

The RealAudio player, available free from Real Networks, enables you to hear audio clips, live and archived radio broadcasts and other sound files through the Web. Many radio stations, such as National Public Radio, and even some television channels, like Cable News Network, now provide their live broadcasts through their websites via RealAudio. A word of warning—this player will attempt to take over your computer, putting links to itself everywhere and associating itself with every type of multimedia file it can think of. Install it only if you really need to do so.

QuickTime

http://www.apple.com/quicktime

The QuickTime viewer, available free from Apple, plays video and audio files through the Web. This is a competing format to other video players, like RealAudio and the Windows Media Player, but favored by many video professionals.

Windows Media Player

http://www.microsoft.com/windows/mediaplayer/default.asp

The Windows Media Player, like the RealAudio and QuickTime viewers, allows users to view video and listen to audio over the Web. Each of these players play their proprietary format as well as some of the other formats.

Multimedia Enhanced Sites

American Sign Language Browser

http://commtechlab.msu.edu/sites/aslweb

QuickTime: From Michigan State University, an online American Sign Language browser. Look up thousands of words and view QuickTime movies illustrating the sign.

BBC World Service

http://www.bbc.co.uk/worldservice/audio

Real Audio: Listen live to the British Broadcasting Company. Areas of interest include news, business, features, science, education, sport, religion, the arts, and youth. Also available in other languages.

broadcast.com

http://www.broadcast.com

Real Audio (usually): A good place to start to search for Internet radio broadcasts. Features a channel guide and a categorical list of links.

Car Talk

http://cartalk.cars.com

The popular weekly NPR program on cars offers all of their shows online. Requires the Real Audio player.

CNN Audioselect

http://www.cnn.com/audio

Real Audio or Windows Media: Catch the latest news online. You can listen to live broadcasts of CNN, CNN Headline News, CNN International, CNN/Sports Illustrated, and CNN en Espanol.

National Public Radio

http://www.npr.org

Real Audio: From the latest hourly news to Morning Edition, All Things Considered, and Car Talk, NPR posts most of their programs on this website for listening at your convenience. They are now streaming their NPR broadcasts live.

Science Friday

http://www.sciencefriday.com

Real Audio: Science Friday, the popular two-hour radio show from National Public Radio, posts all of its broadcasts online. Host Ira Flatow interviews the leading newsmakers in science.

Weather Channel Forecasts

http://www.weather.com/multimedia

Windows Media Player or RealAudio Fast Connection: Watch streaming video forecasts from the Weather Channel.

Music

Bach Central Station

http://www.jsbach.net/bcs/

Everything you always wanted to know about J.S. Bach. There are links to other Bach sites on most every topic. This is a good place to visit to start research or learn about the great composer.

Bands of America

http://www.bands.org/

Bands of America is a leading presenter of music events for high school band students. They sponsor the Grand National Championship, National Concert Band Festival, Summer Band Symposium and other events.

Big Ears

http://www.ossmann.com/bigears/

If you need to train some ears to pitches, this is the place. Big Ears plays an interval and then the user guesses which interval was played. This site uses a Java applet that, once loaded, requires nothing more from you than speakers.

Bulletin Boards for the Music Classroom

http://members.aol.com/jasontracy/bulletinboards.html

If you're stumped for a bulletin board idea, visit this growing site. Categories include boards that brag on your students, boards that teach, seasonal boards, ideas on borders and backgrounds, and others. There are instructions on how to create your own board.

Children's Music Web

http://www.childrensmusic.org/

The Children's Music Web offers the Gazette, their free newsletter, a web guide with links to other music sites in many categories, and short audio programs (in the Real Audio format). They also sponsor a Children's Music Web Awards contest and your classroom can participate or even be a contest judge.

Elementary General Music Teaching & Learning Center

http://www.generalmusic.org/

This is a good music site that features practice and theory. Includes lesson plans and curriculum materials, research information, and an excellent section on research resources.

Energy in the Air: Sounds from the Orchestra

http://tqjunior.thinkquest.org/5116/

Excellent resource on the symphony orchestra. The history of each type of instrument, as well as how sound becomes music, is explained.

Essentials of Music

http://www.essentialsofmusic.com/main.html

From Sony and the W.W. Norton Company, the Essentials of Music is a series designed around the "best classical music" from the Middle Ages to the present. There are almost 70 composer biographies, overviews of each era, a glossary and more than 200 audio excerpts of many pieces of music (Real Audio required).

Fun Music Ideas

http://members.tripod.com/~Trip/newsarchive.html

This site features archived Fun Music Ideas newsletters, which are filled with notes and articles on the teaching of music. The site also offers a very good list of related links with descriptions.

Instrument Encyclopedia

http://www.si.umich.edu/chico/instrument/

A searchable database of more than 140 different musical instruments. This University of Michigan site also offers a glossary, information on other museum collections, and links to related sites.

Internet Resources for Music Scholars

http://hcl.harvard.edu/loebmusic/online-ir-intro.html

This is a very good place to start if you need to do research on music or just want to find what online resources are available. The links are sorted by categories, which include Scholarly Societies, Online Journals and Databases, Music Database, Music Publishers, and Music Information Meta-Sites.

K-12 Resources for Music Educators

http://www.isd77.k12.mn.us/resources/staffpages/shirk/k12.music.html

A list of links for five categories of teachers: Band, Orchestra, Vocal, Classroom, and All Music. Also includes links to sites about music research, newsgroups, and MIDI resources.

KIDiddles

http://www.kididdles.com

The "Musical Mouseum" section of KIDiddles contains an alphabetical listing of hundreds of children's songs (with lyrics, if available). If you can only remember some lyrics but not a title, use their message board to ask others to help.

Land of Music

http://www.landofmusic.com

Music site for elementary grades. Some commercial information. Offers downloadable sing-a-long songs, coloring book pages, and a list of links.

Mozart Project

http://www.mozartproject.org/

This is a great site about Mozart that has matured over the years to become a must-stop for classical music lovers (or even neophytes). It features a long biography of Amadeus, as well as an annotated list of works (some compositions have articles about their history), selected essays, and a nice list of other Mozart-related websites.

Music Education for Young Children

http://www.music4kidsonline.com/meyc/

This site contains music resources for teachers and covers topics like music and the brain, musical development, and teaching ideas. There's also a good list of music organizations and an annotated list of publications.

Music Education Online

http://www.talentz.com/MusicEducation/

This is a very good site full of resources on music and music education. Included are links to grant resources as well as a bookstore, sheet music, and children's CD shop (courtesy of Amazon.com).

Music Education Resource Links

http://www.chapman.edu/soe/faculty/piper/cpiper/musiced.htm

A meta-site of links to curriculum resource for the nine national content standards for music.

Music is (and the Value of Music in Education)

http://www.twinblues.com/

A site that promotes the value of music education to parents (and to other non-believers). Categories of information include Teaching Music, Value of Music, Music and the Brain, Music and Children, and others.

Music Notes

http://library.thinkquest.org/15413/

Billing itself as an "interactive online musical experience," Music Notes is one of the more useful music sites. It features information on the theory, history, and styles of music, as well as a list of links, a nice glossary, and much more.

Music Simply Music

http://www.musicsimplymusic.com/

This commercial site offers many resources for teachers, including a monthly newsletter for teachers, tips for teachers, parents, and students (and tips from students to teachers!), and more.

Music Teachers and Technology

http://www-camil.music.uiuc.edu/tbmi/

Promoting professional development for K-12 music educators, this site from the University of Illinois features examples of technology use in music education. There are also resources for planning and funding, and multimedia examples.

Music Teacher's Resource Site

http://www.mtrs.co.uk/

A United Kingdom site, the MTRS presents information of use for new and experienced teachers of music. You can access the e-mail address of music experts, read equipment and instrument reviews, tips, teacher guides, and much more. Some parts of the site do require a paid subscription.

musicked.com

http://www.musicked.com/

This is a commercial site that does offer valuable free resources (and even more resources with a free registration). You can get critiques on lessons and methods. Use the bulletin board and chat rooms to seek professional guidance or just connect with another music educator.

MusicKit: The Virtual Music Classroom

http://www.musickit.com/

A good site that offers strategies on teaching music, integrating music into the curriculum, and sample activities for kids. Includes planning guides, lesson plans, and classroom resources..

San Francisco Symphony Kids (SFSKIDS)

http://www.sfskids.org

A terrific activity site for kids who want to learn about the instruments of the orchestra, experiment with tempo, rhythm, pitch, harmony, and more, or learn about current events at SFS such as concerts for kids.

MusicStaff.com Teacher Lounge

http://www.musicstaff.com/lounge

Features many articles on the teaching of music, from methods to technology. Also contains a "Students Seeking Teachers" bulletin board, online shopping guide, discussion rooms, and more.

Piano Education Page

http://www.piano.avijon.com/

This is a great site, featuring lots of information for teachers and students of the piano. There are tips on learning to play, reviews of music software, interviews and articles, and much more.

Piano Nanny

http://www.pianonanny.com/

The Piano Nanny features fully interactive online piano lessons. The 34 lessons take about a half hour each and serve as a good introduction to piano playing. For some lessons, you will need the Flash and QuickTime players.

Richard Robinson's Tunebook

http://www.leeds.ac.uk/music/Info/RRTuneBk/

Tunes, and lots of them. Richard Robinson has placed hundreds of tunes from all over the world (but most from Great Britain) on the web. The sheet music is displayed as images, but the download times for the individual songs are very fast. These are tunes, not lyrics.

Rock and Roll Hall of Fame Museum - Lesson Plans

http://www.rockhall.com/programs/plans.asp

A collection of more than 75 lesson plans, covering everything from the Cold War to literacy analysis to feminism. The lesson plans are very detailed.

Science of Sound

http://www.galaxy.net/~k12/sound/

A collection of 17 activities about sound and its relationship to animals, musical instruments, and communications. Each experiment includes a list of needed materials, step-by-step instructions, and teacher notes.

Teaching Ideas

http://www.mmhschool.com/teach/music/music1.html

From the McGraw-Hill School Division, this site has ideas you can use in your teaching, including a "Composer of the Month" feature and ideas for bulletin boards. Be sure to check out the Themes section.

World Wide Web Virtual Library—Classical Music

http://www.gprep.pvt.k12.md.us/classical/

Divided into seven sections, and subdivided within these seven, the WWWVL – Classical Music should be your first stop when searching for websites related to classical music.

Yahoo Directory Music – Classical

http://dir.yahoo.com/entertainment/music/genres/classical/

This helpful directory will lead you websites of any classical genre. Also helpful are the composers, history, artists, chats and forums, MIDI files, and sheet music links.

Organizations

Academy for Educational Development
http://www.aed.org

Activities Integrating Math, Science, & Technology Education
Foundation
http://www.aimsedu.org

American Association for the Advancement of Science
http://www.aaas.org/programs/education/

American Association of Colleges for Teacher Education
http://www.aacte.org

American Association of School Administrators
http://www.aasa.org

American College Testing
http://www.act.org

American Council on Education
http://www.acenet.edu.

American Educational Research Association
http://www.aera.net

American Federation of Teachers
http://www.aft.org

American Library Association
http://www.ala.org

American Literacy Council
http://www.americanliteracy.com/

American Mathematical Society—eMath
http://e-math.ams.org

American Montessori Education
http://www.amshq.org

American Orff-Schulwerk Association
http://www.aosa.org/

Americans for the Arts
http://www.artsusa.org

Association for Career and Technical Education
http://www.avaonline.org

Association for Childhood Education International (ACEI)
http://www.udel.edu/bateman/acei

Association for Educational Communications and Technology
http://www.aect.org

Association for Effective Schools
http://www.mes.org

Association for Supervision and Curriculum Development
http://www.ascd.org

Association for the Advancement of Arts Education
http://www.aaae.org

Association for the Advancement of Computing in Education
http://www.aace.org

Association of American Universities
http://www.tulane.edu/~aau

Association of International Educators (NAFSA)
http://www.nafsa.org

Benton Foundation
http://www.benton.org

Best Practices in Education
http://www.bestpraceduc.org

Center for Accessible Technology
http://www.cforat.org/

Center for Educational Reform
http://www.edreform.com

Center for Educational Innovation
http://www.ceiintl.org

Center for Research on Education, Diversity & Excellence
http://www.crede.ucsc.edu

Center for Science, Mathematics, and Technology Education
http://www.csmate.colostate.edu

Center for the Improvement of Early Reading Achievement
http://www.ciera.org

CEO Forum on Education and Technology
http://www.ceoforum.org

College Art Association
http://www.collegeart.org

Comprehensive Regional Assistance Centers
http://www.ed.gov/EdRes/EdFed/EdTechCtrs.html

Computer 4 Kids
http://www.c4k.org

Computer-Using Educators
http://www.cue.org

Consortium for Equity in Standards and Testing
http://wwwcsteep.bc.edu/ctest

Corporation for National Service
http://www.cns.gov

Council for Aid to Education
http://www.cae.org/

Council for Basic Education
http://www.c-b-e.org

Council for Exceptional Children
http://www.cec.sped.org

Council of Chief State School Officers
http://www.ccsso.org

Council of the Great City Schools
http://www.cgcs.org

Delta Kappa Gamma Society International
http://www.deltakappagamma.org

Drug Abuse Resistance Education (D.A.R.E.)
http://www.dare-america.com

EdWeb: Exploring Technology and School Reform
http://www.edwebproject.org/

Education Commission of the States
http://www.ecs.org/

Education Writers Association
http://www.ewa.org

Education Trust
http://www.edtrust.org

EDUCAUSE
http://www.educause.edu

Educom
http://www.educom.com

ERIC
http://www.indiana.edu/~eric_red

First Book
http://www.firstbook.org

George Lucas Educational Foundation
http://glef.org

I Have a Dream Foundation
http://www.ihad.org

Institute for Responsive Education
http://www.resp-ed.org

Institute for School Innovation
http://www.ifsi.org

Intercollegiate Studies Institute
http://www.isi.org

International Education Financial Aid
http://www.iefa.org

International Literacy Institute
http://www.literacy.org/

International Reading Association
http://www.ira.org

Research & Exchanges Board
http://www.irex.org

International Society for Technology in Education
http://www.iste.org

International Technology Education Association
http://www.iteawww.org

Just Think Foundation
http://www.justthink.org

MacArthur Foundation
http://www.macfdn.org

Math/Science Nucleus Organization
http://www.msnucleus.org

Mathematical Association of America
http://www.maa.org

Milken Family Foundation
http://www.mff.org/

Music Teachers National Association
http://www.mtna.org/

National Academy Foundation (NAF)
http://www.naf.org

National Academy of Child Development
http://www.nacd.org

National Academy of Sciences
http://www4.nas.edu/nas/nashome.nsf

National Alliance of Black School Educators
http://www.nabse.org

National Art Education Association
http://www.naea-reston.org

National Assessment of Educational Progress
http://nces.ed.gov/nationsreportcard/site/home.asp

National Association for Bilingual Education
http://www.nabe.org

National Association for Gifted Children
http://www.nagc.org

National Association for Sport and Physical Education
http://capwiz.com/naspe/home/

National Association for the Education of Young Children
http://www.naeyc.org/

National Association of Biology Teachers
http://www.nabt.org

National Association of Elementary School Principals
http://www.naesp.org/naesp.htm

National Association of Independent Schools
http://www.nais.org

National Association of Early Childhood Specialists in State
Departments of Education
http://ericps.crc.uiuc.edu/naecs/

National Association of Secondary School Principals
http://www.nassp.org

National Association of State Boards of Education
http://www.nasbe.org

National Association of Test Directors
http://www.natd.org

National Center for Early Development & Learning
http://www.fpg.unc.edu/~NCEDL/index.htm

The National Board for Professional Teaching Standards —National
Boards —Professional Certification
National Center for Research on Evaluation, Standards, and Student

Testing
http://cresst96.cse.ucla.edu

National Center for Research on Teacher Learning
http://ncrtl.msu.edu

National Center for the Study of Writing and Literacy
http://www-gse.berkeley.edu/research/NCSWL/csw.homepage.html

National Center on Adult Literacy
http://litserver.literacy.upenn.edu

National Center on Education and the Economy
http://www.ncee.org

National Center on Educational Outcomes
http://www.coled.umn.edu/NCEO

National Center to Improve Practice in Special Education
Through Technology, Media, and Materials (NCIP)
http://www2.edc.org/NCIP

National Council for History Education
http://www.history.org/nche

National Council for Teachers of Mathematics
http://www.nctm.org

National Council for the Social Studies
http://www.ncss.org

National Council of Teachers of English
http://www.ncte.org

National Dropout Prevention Center
http://www.dropoutprevention.org

National Education Association (NEA)
http://www.nea.org

National Educational Service
http://www.nes.org

National Endowment for the Arts
http://arts.endow.gov

National Endowment for the Humanities
http://www.neh.fed.us

National Foundation for Advancement in the Arts
http://www.nfaa.org

National Foundation for Gifted and Creative Children
http://www.nfgcc.org

National Foundation for the Improvement of Education
http://www.nfie.org

National Head Start Association
http://www.nhsa.org/

National High School Association
http://www.nhsa.net

National Institute for Literacy
http://novel.nifl.gov

National Middle School Association
http://www.nmsa.org

National Reading Conference
http://www.iusb.edu/~edud/EleEd/nrc/nrcindex.html

National Research Center on the Gifted and Talented
http://www.ucc.uconn.edu/~wwwgt/nrcgt.html

National School Board Association
http://www.nsba.org

National Science Teachers Association
http://www.nsta.org

National Staff Development Council
http://www.nsdc.org

New American Schools
http://www.naschools.org

Northwest Regional Educational Laboratory
http://www.nwrel.org

Online Computer Library Center
http://www.oclc.org

Parent Teacher Association (PTA)
http://www.pta.org

Phi Delta Kappan
http://www.pdkintl.org

Professional Association for Childhood Education
http://www.pacenet.org

Project Appleseed
http://www.projectappleseed.org

Public Education Network
http://www.publiceducation.org

SMARTer Kids Foundation
http://www.smarterkids.org/

Smithsonian Institution
http://www.si.edu

Society for International Sister Schools
http://www.siss.org

Student Ambassadors Program
http://www.studentambassadors.org

Teach for America
http://www.teachforamerica.org

Teachers of English to Speakers of Other Languages
http://www.tesol.edu

U.S. Charter Schools
http://www.uscharterschools.org

U.S. Network for Educational Information
http://www.ed.gov/NLE/USNEI

U.S. Student Association
http://www.usstudents.org

World Association of Early Childhood Educators
http://www.waece.com/

Publications

Please note:

Some educational journals do not have websites. Many others do have websites but provide little more than subscription information. The publications listed below actually have content on their website. Some magazines may not be suitable for all readers.

Black Collegian

http://www.black-collegian.com

The companion website to the print publication doesn't replicate the magazine— instead it offers employment resources while it bills itself as the "career site for students of color." Users can post resumes, look for jobs in the job bank, search employer profiles, and read articles on career searching.

Black Issues

http://www.blackissues.com

Black Issues' website offers some full-text articles first appearing in the print edition. There are also sections on current news, technology stories, and much more.

Business Week

http://www.businessweek.com

In this online version of the popular business magazine are full-text articles, daily news, and content available only online— a standout site.

Chronicle of Higher Education

http://www.chronicle.merit.edu

This education news site from the country's campuses features seven years of archived back issues. Categories: News, Academe Today (full text), Information Technology, Internet Resources, and Events.

Classroom Compass

http://www.sedl.org/scimath/compass/cchp.html

The Classroom Compass is published by the Southwest Educational Development Laboratory and is intended for teachers interested in improving science and mathematics instruction. Full-text articles are available.

Classroom Connect

http://www.classroom.net

From Classroom Connect magazine, this online site features a superb education-based search engine, a teachers' discussion forum, links to the best education-related websites, and a compendium of online schools—very good site. Categories: Classroom Web, Materials for Educators, Teacher Contacts, Products, and Links.

CopyCat Magazine

http://www.copycatpress.com/

This magazine features ideas and activities for K-3 teachers. Though the site serves mostly to advertise the magazine, some of the pages are available for copying.

TeacherNet

http://www.teachernet.com/

Go to this site for a plethora of teacher resources, such as the latest education news, the Internet site of the week, author interviews, teacher discussions and bulletin boards, links to classroom web pages, information for student teachers, and products for teachers.

Electronic School

http://www.electronic-school.com/

This educational technology magazine was published from 1987 to 2002, and is now archived online. You can view entire issues just by clicking your mouse. Try searching the archives to find specific information.

Early Childhood Today

http://place.scholastic.com/ect

Written for early childhood teachers and published by Scholastic, Early Childhood Today's website features full-length articles, activity ideas, expert advice on development, curriculum suggestions, and more.

Ed.Net.Briefs

http://www.edbriefs.com

Ed.Net Briefs is a weekly e-mail summarizing recent important education news stories. Each story has an accompanying Web link to the full article. Subscribing to this newsletter is a great way to stay current with what's happening in education.

Education Journal Annotations

http://cimc.soemadison.wisc.edu/resources/anno_AB.html

This website provides an annotated list of more than 400 educational journals. The list is arranged alphabetically and includes hyperlinks to the journals' online presence, if they have one.

Education Review

http://www.ed.asu.edu/edrev

Education Review publishes review articles of recently published books on education. The full-length review articles are made available online.

Education Update

http://www.educationupdate.com

Education Update is a free monthly publication that offers articles on education topics in many different categories. Some of the articles are archived on the site.

Education Week on the Web

http://www.edweek.org

One of the best education sites anywhere, it contains current and archived articles, research results, and news and views on education.

Educational Leadership

http://www.ascd.org/cms/index.cfm?TheViewID=353

From the Association for Supervision and Curriculum Development. Selected full-length articles are made available on this website every month.

Electronic Elementary Magazine: "The E-LINK"

http://www.inform.umd.edu/mdk-12/homepers/emag/

This magazine is a nonprofit, educational project that highlights interactive projects and creations of elementary grade students around the world.

Electronic School

http://www.electronic-school.com

Published quarterly as a print and online supplement to The American School Board Journal, this is an excellent magazine site that provides full text articles and information for and about the wired school.

eSchool News online

http://www.eschoolnews.com

A weekly online magazine detailing the latest news in technology/education. It is a companion site to their print publication, but still worthwhile.

From Now On-The Educational Technology Journal

http://fromnowon.org

Free online journal devoted to educational technology issues. Even though the design is somewhat sparse, lengthy, informative issues highlight this journal as one of the better ones on the Internet. Back issues are archives. They also offer free print subscriptions.

Instructor Magazine

http://place.scholastic.com/instructor

Serving elementary teachers nationwide, this website contains everything from strategies for integrating the curriculum and meeting the needs of the kids you teach to professional development opportunities and help with assessment.

Journal of Technology Education

http://scholar.lib.vt.edu/ejournals/JTE/jte.html

The Journal of Technology Education provides a scholarly forum for the discussion of education and technology. Full-length articles are made available in Adobe PDF format.

Learning Magazine

http://www.learningmagazine.com

The Learning Magazine is written for practicing elementary teachers. It offers teaching tips and suggestions, lesson ideas, pointers to good Internet resources, and more.

National Geographic

http://www.nationalgeographic.com

An excellent online version of the magazine, this site offers long stories, beautiful pictures, and resources for both teachers and students.

Principal

http://www.naesp.org/comm/principl.htm

Principal is produced by the National Association of Elementary School Principals. This online companion website offers many of the journal's articles in full-length form.

Scientific American

http://www.sciam.com

An excellent online companion to the popular science magazine, this site has full text-articles with colorful graphics and a searchable index of past articles.

Syllabus Magazine

http://www.syllabus.com/

Explore the use of technology in high schools and universities. Included are case studies, ten years of archived articles, and information on getting published by the magazine.

Teacher Development

http://www.triangle.co.uk/tde/tde-menu.htm

Teacher Development is another journal from the United Kingdom. This one is concerned with professional development. Many full-length articles are available in Adobe PDF format.

Teacher Magazine

http://www.teachermagazine.org/

Part of the Education Week on the website, Teacher Magazine is a slick, very informative online magazine. Changes are made weekly. Categories: Current Events, Research (policy and findings), Editorials, Features (full text).

Teacher Talk

http://education.indiana.edu/cas/tt/tthmpg.html

Teacher Talk is published by the Center for Adolescent Studies at the School of Education, Indiana University, Bloomington, IN. It is a publication for preservice secondary education teachers.

Teaching K–8

http://www.teachingk-8.com

This is another companion website that extends the content of the print magazine. While only a few articles in the print version are available online, there are still enough resources to recommend this website.

Technological Horizons in Education (T.H.E.)

http://www.thejournal.com

News on the world of computers and related technologies focuses on applications that improve teaching and learning for all ages. Categories: T.H.E. Forum, Events and Contests, Professional Development, Grants, Links.

Technology Source

http://ts.mivu.org/

The Technology Source provides full-length articles related to technology and its applications within the fields of teaching and education.

TIME Magazine

http://www.time.com

Part of the huge Pathfinder site, the online version of Time contains most of the printed articles from the weekly, as well as occasional Web specials.

Urban Educator

http://www.cgcs.org/urbaneducator/

The Urban Educator claims to be the "Nation's Voice for Urban Education." This website offers full-text online editions of the publication for free.

U.S. News and World Report

http://www.usnews.com/

Another very good online version of a long-published news magazine, this site also features guides to colleges and graduate programs.

Other Magazines

Atlantic Monthly http://www.theatlantic.com	Harpers http://harpers.org
Billboard http://www.billboard-online.com	Life http://www.lifemag.com
Boston Review http://bostonreview.mit.edu	Mac Today http://www.mactoday.com
Byte http://www.byte.com	Macworld http://macworld.zdnet.com
Car & Driver http://www.caranddriver.com	Men's Health http://www.menshealth.com
Columbia Journalism Review http://www.cjr.org	Money http://money.cnn.com
Computer Shopper http://www.zdnet.com/computershopper	Ms. http://www.msmagazine.com
Consumer Reports http://www.consumerreports.org	Nature http://www.nature.com
Consumers Digest http://www.consumersdigest.com	New Scientist http://www.newscientist.com
Cosmopolitan http://www.cosmomag.com	New York Times Magazine http://www.nytimes.com/library/magazine/home
Discovery http://www.discover.com	Newsweek http://www.newsweek.com
Economist http://www.economist.com	PC World http://www.pcworld.com
Field & Stream http://www.fieldandstream.com	People http://people.aol.com/people
Forbes http://www.forbes.com	Popular Science http://www.popsci.com
Fortune http://www.forbes.com	Reader's Digest http://www.readersdigest.com
Good Housekeeping http://www.goodhousekeeping.com	Salon http://www.salonmagazine.com

Other Magazines *(cont.)*

Saturday Evening Post
http://www.satevepost.org

Slate
http://slate.msn.com/

Sports Illustrated
http://www.cnnsi.com

Wilson Quarterly
http://wwics.si.edu

Wired
http://www.wired.com/wired

Yale Record
http://www.yale.edu/record

ZDNet
http://www.zdnet.com/

Major U.S. Newspapers

Akron Beacon Journal
http://www.beaconjournal.com/

Albuquerque Journal
http://www.abqjournal.com/

Allentown Morning Call
http://www.mcall.com/

Amarillo Globe
http://amarillonet.com/

Arizona Republic
http://www.azcentral.com/news

Arkansas Democrat Gazette
http://www.ardemgaz.com/

Asbury Park Press
http://www.app.com/

Atlanta Journal Constitution
http://www.accessatlanta.com/ajc

Austin Chronicle
http://www.auschron.com

Austin American-Statesman
http://www.austin360.com/

Bakersfield Californian
http://www.bakersfield.com/

Baltimore Sun
http://www.sunspot.net

Baton Rouge Advocate
http://www.theadvocate.com/

Beaumont Enterprise
http://www.beaumontenterprise.com/

Bergen County Record
http://www.bergen.com/

Birmingham News
http://www.bhamnews.com/

Birmingham Post-Herald
http://www.postherald.com/

Booth Newspapers
http://www.mlive.com/

Other Magazines *(cont.)*

Boston Globe
http://www.globe.com

Boston Herald
http://www.bostonherald.com/

Bradenton Herald
http://www.bhip.com/

Buffalo News
http://www.buffnews.com/

Casper Star-Tribune
http://www.trib.com/

Charleston Post Courier
http://www.charleston.net/

Charlotte Observer
http://www.charlotte.com

Chicago Sun-Times
http://www.suntimes.com

Chicago Tribune
http://www.chicagotribune.com

Cincinnati Enquirer
http://gocinci.net/

Cincinnati Post
http://www.cincypost.com

Cleveland Plain Dealer
http://www.cleveland.com/

Colorado Springs Gazette
http://www.gazette.com/

Columbia State
http://www.thestate.com/

Columbus Dispatch
http://www.dispatch.com/

Corpus Christi Caller Times
http://www.caller.com/

Daily Herald (Chicago Suburbs)
http://www.dailyherald.com/

Dallas Morning News
http://www.dallasnews.com

Dayton Daily News
http://www.activedayton.com/ddn/

Denver Post
http://www.denverpost.com

Denver Rocky Mountain News
http://www.rockymountainnews.com/

Des Moines Herald
http://www.desmoinesregister.com/

Detroit Free Press
http://www.freep.com

Detroit News
http://www.detnews.com

Erie Daily Times/Morning News
http://www.goerie.com/

Evansville Courier
http://www.evansville.net/

Flint Journal
http://www.mlive.com/fljournal

Florida Today
http://www.flatoday.com

Fort Lauderdale Sun Sentinel
http://www.sun-sentinel.com/

Fort Wayne News and Sentinel
http://www.news-sentinel.com/ns/

Fort Worth Star-Telegram
http://www.star-telegram.com/

Fresno Bee
http://www.fresnobee.com/

Major U.S. Newspapers

Grand Rapids Press
http://www.mlive.com/grpress/

Green Bay Press Gazette
http://www.greenbaypressgazette.com/

Greensboro News and Record
http://www.greensboro.com/

Hartford Courant
http://www.courant.com

Honolulu Star-Bulletin
http://www.starbulletin.com

Houston Chronicle
http://www.chron.com

Indianapolis Star and News
http://www.starnews.com

Investor's Business Daily
http://www.investors.com/

Jacksonville Times-Union
http://www.jacksonville.com/

Kansas City Star
http://www.kcstar.com

Knoxville News-Sentinel
http://www.knoxnews.com/

Lansing State Journal
http://www.lansingstatejournal.com

Las Vegas Review Journal
http://www.lvrj.com/

Las Vegas Sun
http://www.lasvegassun.com

Lexington Herald Leader
http://www.kentuckyconnect.com/

Little Rock Democrat Gazette
http://www.ardemgaz.com/

Long Beach Press Telegram
http://www.ptconnect.com/

Louisville Courier-Journal
http://www.courier-journal.com/

Los Angeles Daily News
http://www.dailynewslosangeles.com/

Los Angeles Times
http://www.latimes.com

Memphis Commercial Appeal
http://www.gomemphis.com/

Miami Herald
http://www.herald.com

Milwaukee Journal Sentinel
http://www.jsonline.com/

Minnesota Star-Tribune
http://www.startribune.com

New Orleans Times-Picayune
http://www.neworleans.net/

Newark Star Ledger
http://www.nj.com/

New York Daily News
http://www.nydailynews.com

New York Post
http://www.nypostonline.com/

New York Times
http://www.nytimes.com

Newsday
http://www.newsday.com/

Norfolk Virginian Pilot
http://www.pilotonline.com/

Oklahoma City Daily Oklahoman
http://www.oklahoman.com/

Major U.S. Newspapers *(cont.)*

Omaha World-Herald
http://omaha.com/

Orange County Register
http://www.ocregister.com/

Orlando Sentinel
http://www.orlandosentinel.com

Philadelphia Daily News
http://www.philly.com/

Philadelphia Inquirer
http://inquirer.com

Pittsburgh Post-Gazette
http://www.post-gazette.com

Portland Oregonian
http://www.oregonlive.com

Portland (ME) Press Herald
http://www.portland.com/

Providence Journal
http://www.projo.com/

Raleigh News and Observer
http://www.news-observer.com/

Richmond Times Dispatch
http://www.gateway-va.com/

Riverside Press-Enterprise
http://www.inlandempireonline.com/

Rochester Democrat Gazette
http://www.rochesterdandc.com/

Sacramento Bee
http://www.sacbee.com/

Salt Lake City Tribune
http://www.sltrib.com/

San Antonio Express News
http://www.mysanantonio.com/

San Diego Union-Tribune
http://www.uniontribune.com

San Francisco Chronicle
http://www.sfgate.com/

San Francisco Examiner
http://www.examiner.com

San Jose Mercury News
http://www.mercurycenter.com/

Sarasota Herald Tribune
http://www.newscoast.com/

Seattle Post Intelligencer
http://www.seattle-pi.com/

Seattle Times
http://www.seattletimes.com

Spokane Spokesman-Review
http://www.spokane.net/

St. Louis Post Dispatch
http://www.stlnet.com/postnet

St. Paul Pioneer Dispatch
http://www.pioneerplanet.com/

St. Petersburg Times
http://www.sptimes.com/

State Journal (West Virginia)
http://www.statejournal.com

Sun Sentinel (Fort Lauderdale)
http://www.sun-sentinel.com/

Tallahassee Democrat
http://www.tdo.com/

Tacoma News Tribune
http://www.tribnet.com/

Tampa Tribune
http://www.tampatrib.com/

Major U.S. Newspapers *(cont.)*

Tennessean (Nashville)
http://www.tennessean.com/

Toledo Blade
http://www.toledoblade.com/

Tribune Review (Pittsburgh)
http://www.tribune-review.com/trib/

Tulsa World
http://www.tulsaworld.com/

USA Today
http://www.usatoday.com

Wall Street Journal
http://info.wsj.com/cgi-bin/index.cgi

Washington Post
http://www.washingtonpost.com

Washington Times
http://www.washtimes.com

Wilmington News Journal
http://www.delawareonline.com/

Worcester Telegram and Gazette
http://www.telegram.com/

Major International Newspapers

China Daily
http://chinadaily.com.cn

Globe and Mail
http://www.globeandmail.ca

Hong Kong Standard
http://online.hkstandard.com/today

India Express
http://www.expressindia.com

International Herald Tribune
http://www.iht.com

Irish Times
http://www.ireland.com

Japan Times
http://www.japantimes.co.jp

Korea Herald
http://www.koreaherald.co.kr

London Daily Telegraph
http://www.telegraph.co.uk

London Mirror
http://www.mirror.co.uk

Middle East Times
http://metimes.com

Moscow Times
http://www.moscowtimes.ru

Toronto Star
http://www.thestar.com

Reading First

American Association of School Administrators

http://www.aasa.org

The American Association of School Administrators has conveniently posted a list of sites of linked to pages of interest regarding funding, pending legislation, and the latest information on the topic of Reading First implementation. Be sure to check out their links to information on scientifically-based research as well.

The Book Hive

http://www.bookhive.org/

The Book Hive is a resource for children's literature and books. It has information on a variety of books for children from birth to age 12. Categories include award-winning books, beginning chapter books, fantasy, folklore, non-fiction, and more.

Children's Book Council

http://www.cbcbooks.org

According to the site, the Children's Book Council (CBC) "is a non-profit trade organization dedicated to encouraging literacy and the use and enjoyment of children's books, and is the official sponsor of Young People's Poetry Week and Children's Book Week each year. The Council's Members include U.S. publishers and packagers of trade books for children and young adults."

Find on this site information about new book releases, a bimonthly showcase of books, and information about professional education programs.

Early Reading First

http://www.ed.gov/programs/earlyreading/index.html

The Early Reading First program's purpose is to prepare children entering kindergarten with needed reading skills. At this site, you can learn more about the initiative and the grant competition.

Education Place's Reading/Language Arts Center

http://www.eduplace.com/rdg/

This site provides information on the Reading First initiative as well as printable resources, an online book group, and collaborative reading projects developed by teachers.

Education Week

http://www.edweek.org

Education Week on the Web is always a worthwhile site to have bookmarked in your list of favorites. Currently, you will find a particularly interesting article written in layman's terms to review the key points of the Reading First initiative. Look for the headline No Child Left Behind on their homepage. If you don't find it there, type those words into the site's search engine to retrieve the article from their archives.

ERIC Clearinghouse on Reading, English, and Communication

http://www.indiana.edu/~eric_rec/

The ERIC Clearinghouse has searchable educational materials for reading. Included is News About Reading, Bookstore, Lesson Plans, Family Info Center, Online Education, Web Resources, and Q & A Services.

Helping Your Child Become a Reader

http://www.ed.gov/pubs/parents/Reader/index.html

Find in this helpful publication activities that teachers and parents can use to get children to become readers. As some of the activities start at age "birth," it's clear that not all of them involve actually reading, but getting excited about language and learning. Also provided is information about computers and using libraries.

Home for the Holidays...Reading Together

http://www.ed.gov/inits/holidays/index.html

This site provides tips on getting kids to read at home and during school holidays. Find here links to suggested reading lists, a bookmark-making activity, and tips to provide to parents on reading well with their children.

How Do I Know a Good Early Reading Program When I See One?

http://www.ed.gov/inits/rrrl/guide.html

This guide for parents on what to look for in a good early reading program can also be used by educators designing their reading programs. It has tips on the type and amount of extra help to provide to students who fall behind.

International Reading Association

http://www.reading.org/focus/nclb.html

The International Reading Association maintains this portion of their website with updated links to the various resources containing information relevant to the Reading First initiatives in the No Child Left Behind legislation. The IRA continually adds new materials as they become available.

CyberGuides: Teacher Guides and Student Activities

http://www.sdcoe.k12.ca.us/score/cyberguide.html

Visit this terrific resource to find all the tools you need for teaching around core works of literature. Student and teacher editions, standards, websites, and a rubric are included in each CyberGuide. The list of literature for each grade level is quite extensive.

Making a Difference Means Making it Different: Honoring Children's Rights to Excellent Reading Instruction

http://www.reading.org/positions/MADMMID.html

This page from the International Reading Association summarizes its position on children's rights to reading instruction. Included are the right to early reading instruction, reading assessment that is personalized for their strengths and weaknesses, and equal access to technology used for the improvement of reading instruction. A description of these rights can be viewed online or downloaded in PDF format.

National Institute for Literacy

http://www.nifl.gov/

The National Institute for Literacy maintains a website where many documents on the Reading First initiative are available to be read online. Of particular interest to teachers is the 2001 publication, Put Reading First: The Research Building Blocks for Teaching Children to Read.

National Reading Panel

http://www.nationalreadingpanel.org/

The National Reading Panel has numerous publications and materials available for understanding how to improve reading instruction. Along with summary reports and research findings, this site offers a video developed by the National Reading Panel entitled, "Teaching Children to Read."

No Child Left Behind

http://www.nochildleftbehind.gov/next/overview/presentation/index.html

To understand the Reading First initiative, you must first get a sense of the No Child Left Behind Act of 2001. For a quick overview of the key points of this legislation, you can click through a series of slides at the No Child Left Behind website.

Phonemic Awareness and the Teaching of Reading
http://www.reading.org/positions/phonemic.html

The International Reading Association published these findings on the importance of phonics and phonemic awareness in the teaching of reading to children. It suggests a teaching strategy that balances language awareness with comprehension and enjoyment. The information can be viewed online or downloaded in PDF format.

Preventing Reading Difficulties in Young Children
http://stills.nap.edu/html/prdyc/

This publication discusses the process of learning to read and identifies the predictors of reading difficulties. Find out when to intervene and when and how to act with pre-kindergarten, kindergarten, and primary-grade age children. The sections of the publication include Introduction to Reading, Who Are We Talking About?, Prevention and Intervention, and Knowledge into Action.

Read, Think, Write
http://www.readwritethink.org/

ReadWriteThink is a partnership between the International Reading Association (IRA), the National Council of Teachers of English (NCTE), and the MarcoPolo Education Foundation. The stated goal of this site is to provide educators and students with access to the highest quality practices and resources in reading and language arts instruction through free, Internet-based content.

Reading is Fundamental
http://www.rif.org/

RIF is involved in developing programs to prepare and motivate children to read. The RIF Reading Planet has interactive and motivating activities for kids of all ages and their families. A downloadable activity calendar provides reading activities for every day of the month.

Ready to Read*Ready to Learn

http://www.ed.gov/inits/rrrl/index.html

This site has First Lady Laura Bush's Educational Initiatives, with sections on Bringing What Works to Parents; The Tools to Teach What Works; Recruiting the Best and the Brightest; and Strong Teachers, Strong Families, Strong Students. The information can also be downloaded in PDF format.

Starting Out Right

http://bob.nap.edu/readingroom/books/sor/

Starting Out Right is a book about reading success for children, and this site has excerpts from the book with valuable information that you can use in your classroom today. There are sections on Growing Up to Read from birth to age four, Becoming Real Readers from kindergarten to third grade, and Preventing Reading Difficulties.

State Information—No Child Left Behind

http://nclb.gov/next/where/statecontacts.html

Click on your state and find a list of representatives and educational resources in your area. You can also find out how your state is doing in standardized test scores.

Technology Briefs for NCLB Planners

http://www.neirtec.org/products/techbriefs/default.asp

The Northeast and Islands Regional Technology Consortium, or NEIRTEC, maintains this site as an information repository of briefs helpful to state and local technology planners. These briefs outline the pertinent information that must be included in any requests for funding made available as part of the 2002 No Child Left Behind (NCLB) Act.

Research and Reference Resources

Acronym Finder

http://www.acronymfinder.com

This is a very good database that has definitions for more than 240,000 acronyms. Each definition has a link to Amazon, which is a little ridiculous, but this a useful resource nonetheless.

American Fact Finder

http://factfinder.census.gov/servlet/BasicFactsServlet

From the U.S. Census Bureau, this website presents statistical information on population and housing, social characteristics, labor force and employment, and income and poverty status. This site gets better each year as more information is added to it.

AskERIC Home Page

http://ericir.syr.edu

ERIC is the Educational Resources Information Center (ERIC), a federally-funded national information system that provides, through its 16 subject-specific clearinghouses, associated adjunct clearinghouses, and support components, a variety of education-related services and products.

Bartleby.com

http://www.bartleby.com

This is the home page for many different reference titles, including Gray's Anatomy, American Heritage Dictionary, Book of English Usage, and Oxford Shakespeare. All are fully searchable and free.

Best Information on the Net

http://www.sau.edu/Internet/

A Top Five site by most accounts. Well-organized portal for research resources on the Internet. Information on academic and popular issues. If you need an idea for something to write about, check out the Hot Paper Topics section.

Child Stats

http://childstats.gov/

From the Forum on Child and Family Statistics, this site offers easy access to federal and state statistics and reports on children and their families.

CIA World Fact Book

http://www.cia.gov/cia/publications/factbook/

An incredible free resource for students and teachers (and anyone interested in other countries). From Afghanistan to Zimbabwe, and all countries in between, the CIA presents a wealth of facts at your fingertips.

Dictionary.com

http://www.dictionary.com

Just what the name implies, an online dictionary. Also offers a dictionary of English jargon and writing resources (grammar, usage, style, etc.).

Education Planet

http://www.educationplanet.com

Education Planet, like Education World, is a search engine for education-related websites. This site features sections on top sites, most popular searches, current education news, and much more. It's one of the best sites in the book.

Education World Search Engine

http://www.education-world.com

A Yahoo!-like search engine dedicated to educators and students. There are education news, chat forums, education site reviews, and links to commercial sites.

Educational Policy Analysis Archives

http://epaa.asu.edu/epaa/

Hosted by Arizona State University's College of Education, this archive is full of articles on educational policy. You can browse the abstracts, download the full articles, and even submit your own paper.

EduHound.com

http://www.eduhound.com/

EduHound.com maintains a very big meta-list of education-related websites. The links are listed by category and are easy to find.

EdWeb: Exploring Technology and School Reform

http://www.edwebproject.org

With EdWeb, you can hunt down online educational resources around the world, learn about trends in education policy and information infrastructure development, examine success stories of computers in the classroom, and much, much more.

Electronic Reference Formats from the APA

http://www.apa.org/journals/webref.html

This online guide, from the American Psychological Association, gives details and examples on how to cite resources from e-mail communications, a website, documents on a website, and articles and abstracts from electronic databases.

Encarta

http://encarta.msn.com

Encarta is the popular encyclopedia from Microsoft. This online companion offers many of the same articles, though not as in depth as the CD-Rom.

Encyclopaedia Britannica

http://www.britannica.com/

Now free, the venerable encyclopedia offers complete access to its huge database of information.

Encyclopedia.com from Electric Library

http://www.encyclopedia.com

A searchable and free encyclopedia with more than 5,000 articles. Many articles, though short, include related Internet sites. If you choose to subscribe to the pay service, more articles are made available. The site also offers a thesaurus, dictionaries, and an almanac.

Fedstats

http://www.fedstats.gov

Fedstats is a one-stop clearinghouse of statistical information kept by more than 100 agencies of the Federal Government.

Grammar Bytes

http://www.chompchomp.com

This interactive grammar review offers an index of grammar terms, interactive exercises, and a short list of grammar rules with explanations. It is well suited for the young writer.

Homework Central

http://www.homeworkcentral.com

Divided into three sections (grades 1-6, middle & high school, college & beyond) this site is a categorical list (like Yahoo!) of websites. Designed to help students find more information about their homework subject—not to do their homework for them.

Impact of Technology

http://www.mcrel.org/topics/productDetail.asp?productID=108

An excellent resource that features complete articles, surveys, etc., that explore the impact of technology in the classroom, this should be your first stop if you want to do research about technology and education.

Infonation

http://www.un.org/Pubs/CyberSchoolBus/infonation/e_infonation.htm

Infonation allows users to compare and contrast demographic information from all of the world's countries. Users select countries, then select information to compare—an easy-to-read table is then presented.

Information Please

http://www.infoplease.com

A huge, huge repository of information. Nicely organized and searchable, too. Features many almanacs, lists, and just about anything else you can think of.

Internet FAQ Archive

http://www.faqs.org

This site represents an attempt to keep track of all the FAQs on the Internet, of which there are thousands. A FAQ on just about anything is accessible from here.

Kelley Blue Book

http://www.kbb.com

We all know that teachers have a lot of money and are always in the market for a new or used car. This site will give you pricing information on new cars and trade-in values for used cars.

Library of Congress

http://marvel.loc.gov

From the biggest library in the world comes perhaps one of the best websites ever. Search for legislative information, browse exhibits, or use their research search tool to search other Internet sites.

LibrarySpot

http://www.libraryspot.com

Another good place to start research. Categorical links to reference sites, library information and more. Most information is off-site.

Lookup Zip+4

http://www.usps.gov/ncsc/lookups/lookup_zip+4.html

If you need a Zip Code, or the last four digits of a nine-digit zip code, this free database will give it to you.

McGuffey Reader

http://digital.library.pitt.edu/cgi-bin/nietz.pl?notisid=00ACH0530m&type=header

Want to get an idea of what elementary education was like 150 years ago? You'll be surprised as you page through this book. The McGuffey Reader was THE American textbook, selling millions throughout the years.

My Virtual Reference Desk

http://www.refdesk.com

Links to U.S. and world newspapers, 200 search engines, 40 categories of encyclopedias, and much, much more.

National Center for Education Statistics

http://www.ed.gov/NCES

The National Center for Education Statistics fulfills a Congressional mandate to collect, collate, analyze, and report complete statistics on the condition of American education, conduct and publish reports, and review and report on education activities internationally.

National Public School Locator

http://nces.ed.gov/ccdweb/school/

A database containing information on all of the public and private schools and school districts in the country. The database is provided by the U.S. Department of Education and offers general descriptions, data on students and staff, and fiscal data.

One Look Dictionaries

http://www.onelook.com

This dictionary has almost 5 million words and acronyms compiled from more than 800 dictionaries. Easy to use and difficult to stump.

Online English Grammar

http://www.edufind.com/english/grammar

A great online grammar book. Searchable alphabetically or by topic. Also features sound files for pronunciation rules, software reviews, free interactive tests, and even a list of open employment positions.

Online Medical Dictionary

http://www.graylab.ac.uk/omd

Search for everything medical at this site. The definitions are all hyperlinked, making subject searches easier to do.

Periodic Table of the Elements (Webelements)

http://www.webelements.com

Excellent use of the hyperlinked medium. Click on an element in the table and get all kinds of information about it, including a description and historical facts.

Practical Assessment Research and Evaluation

http://ericae.net/pare/

This online journal provides educators with syntheses of some of the latest research and ideas about issues and practice in education in the hope of having a positive impact on assessment, evaluation, and teaching practice.

Roget's Thesaurus

http://www.thesaurus.com

A complete online searchable Roget's Thesaurus. Perfect for finding that one special word.

Strunk's Elements of Style

http://www.bartleby.com/141

The complete version of Elements of Style, the handbook of writers for decades. Presented in an easily navigable format.

U.S. Historical Documents

http://www.law.ou.edu/hist

From the Magna Carta to President Clinton's second inaugural address and everything in between, this site has the historical record of the United States in hypertext format. Very nice!

Webopedia

http://www.pcwebopedia.com

Webopedia is a hyperlinked encyclopedia of computer terms. Each definition comes complete with a set of related terms and relevant web pages.

World Wide Web Virtual Library

http://vlib.org/Overview.html

A very comprehensive site featuring links (within categories) to virtually hundreds of thousands of websites. Must be seen to be believed.

World-Wide Web Virtual Library - Education

http://www.csu.edu.au/education/library.html

A very good site. The education section of the WWW Virtual Library. This site provides very extensive resources on many topics.

Your Dictionary

http://www.yourdictionary.com/

Hundreds of dictionaries in hundreds of different languages, from Afrikaans to Yemba. Also includes thesauri, online grammars, etymological dictionaries and much more.

Science

An Inquirer's Guide to the Universe

http://sln.fi.edu/planets/planets.html

If your students are interested in the universe (or even if they don't know that they're interested in the universe), point them to this excellent site. It is devoted to space, science fact and fiction, and writing about space (students can post writings on the site). Also contains suggestions on how to use the guide in the classroom.

Ask Dr. Science

http://www.ducksbreath.com

Ask Dr. Science is a humorous, yet not quite scientific, site where Dr. Science answers your science questions, such as why doesn't a boiled egg turn vaporous.

Ask Science Questions

http://www.sciencepage.org/question.htm

This site provides links to other sites where you can send in questions to be answered by scientists. Included is everything from Ask an Antarctic Expert to Ask a Volcanologist.

Batting Cage

http://tqd.advanced.org/11902/physics/batting.html

Fun and interesting way to learn physics. Divided into three levels of difficulty. Explains in plain English the laws of physics and terms such as velocity, grade, and gravity.

Bill Nye, the Science Guy

http://www.billnye.com

A good science site, if somewhat slow to load at times, that uses Flash to offer interactive daily activities and questions of the week as well as information on the television show.

Biology Project

http://www.biology.arizona.edu

An online interactive resource for learning biology. Covers biochemistry, cell biology, chemicals & human health, developmental biology, human biology, immunology, genetics and molecular biology.

Brain Pop

http://www.brainpop.com

Brain Pop presents hundreds of interactive lessons in health, technology, and science. The site is very colorful and uses great Shockwave movies.

Bugs in the News!

http://people.ku.edu/~jbrown/bugs.html

Bugs in the News, by Jack Brown at the University of Kansas, spotlights bugs that have made the news for good or bad. Most of the site is comprised of well-written articles probably best-suited for at least high school students.

Composting in Schools

http://www.cfe.cornell.edu/compost/schools.html

This website from Cornell gives you all the information you'll need to start your own compost project, either indoors or outside, and how you teach about waste management and other subjects.

Cool Science for Curious Kids

http://www.hhmi.org/coolscience

Presented by the Howard Hughes Medical Institute, this "cool science" site helps students explore the biology of plants and animals. Includes instructions on making science projects and even hints for parents.

Dinsoauria

http://www.dinosauria.com

This site features an excellent gallery of dinosaur images. The text is more suited for high school students, but elementary school students will love the pictures.

Dinosauricon

http://dinosauricon.com/

There's a lot of information on dinosaurs here, enough to keep any student busy for a long time. The site offers a genus list that offers a complete list of all dinosaurs, a large art gallery, dinosaurs by continent, and, of course, a list of related links. This is probably best for upper-level students.

Electronic Zoo

http://netvet.wustl.edu/e-zoo.htm

This is a huge repository of animal information. The Zoo is organized by animal, and clicking on an animal gives you a long list of links to related sites on the Web. Also featured are veterinary information and animal organization information.

Science: A Curriculum Guide for the Elementary Level

http://www.sasked.gov.sk.ca/docs/elemsci/elemsci.html

The aim of these science units from Saskatchewan Education is to develop scientific literacy in students grades 1-5. There are also suggestions on how to organize your classroom to optimize science activities, conduct high-quality assessment, and plan a science unit.

Exploratorium

http://www.exploratorium.edu

Another excellent science-based site, it has plenty of Science Explorer activities for students, including light and shadows and a virtual cow's eye dissection lesson. New activities are updated often.

Explore Zone

http://www.space.com/

Now called SPACE.com, this site offers science news focusing on the Earth, Space, and Weather sciences. Click the SpaceViews tab to see amazing pictures of all things space-related.

ENC Online: ENC Features: Lessons & Activities

http://www.enc.org/features/lessonplans/?ls=fe

This is the place to go for easy access to science and math lessons on the Internet. Web sites offering science and math lessons have been categorized by topic. You can also find lessons by using the search engine.

Exploring Leonardo

http://www.mos.org/sln/Leonardo/LeoHomePage.html

If your students think the only Leonardo was that guy in that movie about a boat, they'll need to come here. Leonardo da Vinci was an inventor, artist and a scientist before his time. This is a well-designed, informative, and beautifully illustrated website.

Franklin Institute Science Museum

http://sln.fi.edu/tfi/welcome.html

This is a beautiful site with many science resources. You can take virtual tours of many exhibits, check out units of study guides on living things and wind, and even pose a science question to an "expert."

Globe

http://www.globe.gov

Global Learning and Observations to Benefit the Environment (GLOBE) is a worldwide network of students, teachers, and scientists working together to study and understand the global environment. GLOBE students make a core set of environmental observations at or near their schools and report their data via the Internet—a very good site.

Goddard's Science Question of the Week

http://www.gsfc.nasa.gov/science.html

From the Goddard Space Center, a weekly science question and answer. Recommended that you give the question on Monday, the answer on Friday. Includes the last three years' worth of questions and answers.

Great Plant Escape

http://www.urbanext.uiuc.edu/gpe

The Great Plant Escape presents plant life science lessons. Students can help the detective unlock the mystery of plant life. There are six "cases," all dealing with plant biology. Good for upper elementary. Includes a teacher's guide and an illustrated glossary.

Heart Preview Gallery

http://sln2.fi.edu/biosci/preview/heartpreview.html

Everything that relates to the heart. There are teacher resource materials, x-ray images, sounds of the heart, poetry, music, a tour and more. The site offers many video clips, even one of an open heart surgery.

Virtual Frog Dissection

http://www-itg.lbl.gov/ITG.hm.pg.docs/dissect/info.html

This is one of the most visited sites on the Web and still the best way to dissect a frog. Using multimedia and other technologies, students can virtually dissect a frog by following along with the step-by-step directions. The video clips do a good job of illustrating the process.

JASON Project

http://www.jasonproject.org

A great site, it is one for all teachers! The JASON Foundation for Education, which was founded to administer the project, sponsors an annual scientific expedition which is the focus of an original curriculum developed for grades 4 through 8. During the expedition, students can take part in a live, interactive program. Categories: Past Expeditions, Newsroom, Press Kits

Kids World 2000

http://now2000.com/kids/

A "guide for the young cyber-traveler" that includes links to museums, zoos and aquariums, science, sports and geography sites.

MAD Scientist Network

http://www.madsci.org

Featuring science lessons, exhibits, and experiments, this site covers physics, biology, chemistry, and other areas. It is useful for teachers and students.

Meteorology Guide

http://ww2010.atmos.uiuc.edu/(Gh)/guides/mtr/home.rxml

The Online Meteorology Guide is a collection of Web-based instructional modules that use multimedia technology and the dynamic capabilities of the Web—very comprehensive. Probably better suited for upper-level students.

NASA Quest

http://quest.arc.nasa.gov/livefrom/livefrom.html

NASA links to the current educational activities they are sponsoring and includes archived lessons, information about the initiative, and a lot more.

NASA Spacelink: An Aeronautics & Space Resource for Educators

http://spacelink.msfc.nasa.gov

Another site from NASA, this one is devoted to space flight. It offers curriculum and instructional materials in math, history, geography, and language arts and also contains links to other aerospace resources.

Nine Planets

http://seds.lpl.arizona.edu/nineplanets/nineplanets/nineplanets.html

The Nine Planets is a multimedia tour of the solar system that includes information on more than just the nine planets, with excellent images and lots of information. Another good part of the site is the glossary, which is useful for anyone studying space and the planets.

Nobel Prize Internet Archive

http://nobelprizes.com/nobel/nobel.html

Features up-to-date information on the latest Nobel Prize winners, as well as biographical information on all the past winners.

Periodic Table of the Elements (Webelements)

http://www.webelements.com

Excellent use of the hyperlinked medium. Click on an element in the table and get all kinds of information about it, including a description and historical facts.

Physics 2000

http://www.colorado.edu/physics/2000/

Physics 2000, from the University of Boulder, offers a fun and informative interactive journey through modern physics. This highly awarded site offers interactive experiments and easy-to-read, yet educational, text. Definitely a must-see site.

Physlink

http://www.physlink.com/

Physlink is a physics portal pointing to news articles and websites related to physics. The site features an Ask the Experts section and information on the history of physics. There are also many educator resources on the site.

Rainforest Australia

http://rainforest-australia.com

Australia has rain forests, too, and this website offers the viewer text and images covering the many different facets of the forest. This site serves as a gateway for a commercial outfit but the articles and images are educational nonetheless.

Satellites and Satellite Trackers

http://liftoff.msfc.nasa.gov/academy/rocket_sci/satellites/

There are more than 2,500 satellites orbiting the Earth and somebody has to keep track of them. NASA does, and students can use this site to help keep watch. They can also see exactly where the shuttle is and learn what bright objects will be over their heads tonight.

Science Learning Network

http://www.sln.org

Funded by the National Science Foundation, the Science Learning Network (SLN) is an online community of educators, students, schools, science museums, and other institutions demonstrating a new model for inquiry science education. You'll find many resources to use in your classroom.

Sea and Sky

http://www.seasky.org

This huge site, devoted to astronomy and oceanography, features image galleries, games, articles, and links to other like resources on the Web.

Simplified Science Animations

http://www.geocities.com/Athens/Olympus/5297

Created by a high school science teacher in Michigan, this collection of more than 20 science animations illustrates cell basics, nuclear fission, bat sonar, etc. Best of all, he has given permission for you to download and use them (they will work in PowerPoint presentations).

Solar System Simulator

http://space.jpl.nasa.gov

By making a few choices, you can get a look at many of the planetary bodies of the universe as seen from many other bodies of the universe at any given day or time.

Soundry

http://library.thinkquest.org/19537/

If you're going to conduct some lessons on sound, check out the Soundry before you start your lesson planning. This often-recognized site is the product of three students and contains information on the physics of sound, how the ear works, and a time line of the recording of sound.

Super Science Home Page

http://www.sci-ed-ga.org/modules/k6/ss

This site is designed to encourage kids, teachers, and parents to do scientific experiments. It includes ideas for experiments, advice on performing and presenting experiments, an online contest, information on exciting books and multimedia titles, and information on applying for a new science grant for teachers.

Tech Museum of Innovation

http://www.thetech.org/exhibits_events/online

Using Shockwave and RealAudio (see multimedia section of this book for more information), the Tech Museum presents online exhibits illustrating the making of a satellite, climbing Mt. Everest, exploring earthquakes, and other science-related subjects.

Virtual Fetal Pig Dissection

http://www.whitman.edu/biology/vpd/

This site offers a useful alternative or enhancement to some biology classes that still do pig dissections. The site is very graphic and the dissection is enhanced by the use of online quizzes.

Windows to the Universe

http://www.windows.ucar.edu

Windows to the Universe is an excellent website offering resources on the earth and space sciences. Students can learn about space, space weather, and the solar system. This site is very extensive and one of the best space sites around.

World Wide Web Virtual Library- Science

http://vlib.org/Science.html

Another WWW Virtual Library, this one devoted to Science, with separate sections for biosciences, chemistry, physics, and more.

Yucky, Gross & Cool Body

http://yucky.kids.discovery.com/body/

As the title implies, this science site delves into areas that some people would just as soon not think about. But the site is well done. Its aim at getting kids interested in science by talking about bodily fluids and the like is probably successful.

Searching the Web

As anyone who has ever searched the Web knows, it can be difficult (or impossible) to find what you are looking for (after all, that's why this book was written). However, by knowing the rules that search engines use, you can greatly increase your searching success.

Search engines do not know of every page on the Web. In a study published in the journal, Nature, in 1999, it was estimated that, at best, search engines may catalogue less than 20% of all web pages. Studies done since then have delivered even worse statistics. The best estimates of how many web pages there are is more than two billion. Obviously, then, the search engines cannot possibly show you all there is out there. So, how to find what you are looking for? One way is to not even go to the search engines. Start at sites that are related to the one you are looking for. Many sites offer a "links" section that has pointers to related sites. Another good way is to look in the Public and Private Organizations section of this book and find a website of an organization related to the subject you are searching for. Go to the organization's website and look for related links.

If all else fails, search engines can be helpful, especially if you know how to use them. To use them efficiently, you'll need to know how they operate. Below is relevant information and hints when using some of the more popular search engines.

Directories

Some search engines employ people to go to sites, determine what the site is about, then list the site in the search engine's categorical or hierarchical listing. The most well-known search engine that uses this method is Yahoo! This is great for being able to narrow down the categories and subcategories until you find what you need, as long as you know in which category the site is listed. If you don't, you can search the categories and subcategories (that's why even categorical/hierarchical search engines have a search tool on their page). What isn't great is that when you use the search tool, you are only searching the categories. You are not searching the Web. Additionally, since hundreds of thousands of web pages are added to the Web each week, no company can employ enough people to go to those pages and efficiently categorize them for inclusion. Finally, when a web page changes, the site's author must submit the page address for a re-categorization (if necessary) and not many have the time to do this.

Directory search engines are best used when searching for general information (subjects that fit nicely into a category) or for businesses. So if you use Yahoo! or Looksmart to search for Education, you'll find many listings other than title. However, if you use the same search engine to look for a quote from Lawrence Cremin on Education that you saw once in the middle of some web page, you may come up empty.

Full Web Search

There are other search engines that make an attempt to catalogue the entire Web (although, like I said, they may get 20% of the Web, tops). These engines send out "spiders," computer software robots that jump from one page to the next. Some read just the page titles and META tags (META tags are HTML codes put in the page by web developers that give a description of the page and some keywords— these tags are invisible to users). Others attempt to index all the text on a page. They then file away the text and the page's address in the system.

There are some minor flaws in this system, not the least of which is that quantity does not equate with quality. Doing a search for Education on a popular web search engine like Hotbot will get you more than 3.2 million results, a few too many for most people to wade through. Additionally, there are some web developers that will do anything to get eyes on their pages. They will use tricks, such as including hundreds of words in the keywords META tag, most of which has nothing to do with their web page.

Tips:

Narrow your focus. Don't search under Education when what you are really interested in is teacher education programs in Wyoming. Also, use quotes (" ") when specify that you are looking for a phrase. Many directory search engines will accept submissions in quotes. For example, let's say you are searching for teacher education programs in Wyoming. Using Hotbot, if you type teacher education Wyoming, you will get approximately 4,800 results. This is better than the 3.2 million results you got for Education, but still far too many. To get better results, search for the phrase "teacher education" and Wyoming together by submitting your search like this: "teacher education" Wyoming. This narrows the results to 60, a far more reasonable return.

Be aware of how search engines work. This is especially true when you know just what you are looking for. For example, I recently did a search for a page I had visited a few months ago but had neglected to bookmark. I did, however, remember the title of the page. Some search engines, like Yahoo! and HotBot, allow you to search titles of pages by prefacing your search terms with title: This tells the search engine to search the titles, not the text on the pages.

Read the rules. Most search engines provide hints on how to get better results. Usually, clicking on "Advanced Search" will let you specify more options for your search. For example, Hotbot's Advanced Search function will let you specify what words must be on the page, what words must not be on the page, which domain to search (edu for educational site, com for commercial sites), and even what language to search in. Other search engines offer similar options and, when used wisely, can result in much better returns.

Use the tricks. Some directory search engines, like Yahoo, offer Advanced Search options that let you specify a phrase, rather than a group of words. So, for example, searching for teacher education Wyoming will get more than 8,000 results. Doing an advanced search for "teacher education" Wyoming narrows the results to less than 1,000, still a lot but better than 8,000.

Finally, if you find all search engines lacking, there is an alternative (besides buying this book, which you did—thank you). You can obtain software programs that will do searches of multiple search engines at the same time. One popular program is Copernic (free for Windows—no Mac version) available at http://www.copernic.com. Copernic will submit each search to many different search engines at once and then create a web page listing the results. Copernic does contain advertising that cannot be turned off (which is probably why it is a free download).

Search Engines

To determine which search engine is best, give them all a try. Many people are very loyal to one particular search engine based on past performance. Indeed, taking the time to learn the ins and outs of one or two search engines can make a believer out of the user. So you should take the time to try them all and see which one works best for you.

Google

http://www.google.com

Far and away the first choice of most web veterans, Google has won the hearts and minds of knowledgeable surfers everywhere. While other search sites are plagued by pop-up ads and paid placement, Google keeps it simple and effective. To take full advantage of the site, look in the advanced features section, and try out the Google toolbar.

Popular Search Engines

AltaVista
http://www.altavista.com

Ask Jeeves
http://www.askjeeves.com

Direct Hit
http://www.directhit.com

Excite
http://www.excite.com

Fast Search
http://www.alltheweb.com

Google
http://www.google.com

Hotbot
http://www.hotbot.com

Looksmart
http://www.looksmart.com

Lycos
http://www.lycos.com

MSN Web Search
http://search.msn.com

Netscape Search
http://search.netscape.com

Northern Light
http://www.northernlight.com

SEARCH.COM
http://search.cnet.com

Snap
http://www.snap.com

WebCrawler
http://webcrawler.com

Yahoo!
http://www.yahoo.com

Specialized Search Engines

Education World

http://www.education-world.com

Education World is a search engine for education-related sites. These websites are submitted to the engine and then placed in categories (you can also search all the categories). Monthly "best" sites are picked and viewing these lists can be a good way to find quality sites.

Internet FAQ Archive

http://www.faqs.org

This site represents an attempt to keep track of all the Frequently Asked Questions (FAQs) on the Web and the USENET, of which there are thousands. A FAQ on just about anything is accessible from here.

Education Planet

http://www.educationplanet.com

Education Planet, like Education World, is a search engine for education-related websites. This site features sections on Top Sites, most popular searches, current education news, and much more. One of the best sites in this book.

Sites For Students

Amusement Park Physics

http://www.learner.org/exhibits/parkphysics/

This is an excellent site that teaches science by looking at the physics of the popular park rides. Students can even get a chance to build their own coasters.

Animals Myths and Legends

http://members.ozemail.com.au/~oban/

Oban the Knowledge Keeper has been around for a while, and he and his fellow storytellers take students through the world of myths and legends where they'll learn the importance of these stories to the Aboriginal peoples of Australia and other cultures. Story pages fit nicely on the screen and include some illustrations. The playroom offers coloring pages and a crossword.

Ask Earl

http://www.yahooligans.com/content/ask_earl

Each day, Earl answers a question posed by students. The answers are sometimes humorous, often educational, and provide links to related online resources. This could be a great way to start or end the school day.

Great Web Sites for Kids

http://www.ala.org/greatsites

This subject directory created by the American Library Association is a terrific site for your students to use when searching for information on the Internet.

BBC Schools Online

http://www.bbc.co.uk/schools

The British Broadcasting Company has created a wonderful resource you can share with your students. Each site included here has a recommended age level and promises an educational adventure.

Create Your Own Newspaper

http://crayon.net

A free site, CRAYON lets kids (and adults) create their very own newspapers. With downloadable links to real newspaper and broadcast stories and graphics, this is a great site to use to experiment and learn the ins and out of journalism.

CyberKids Home

http://www.cyberkids.com

This is a site designed for younger kids to publish their artwork, writing, and even music (in mid format, only). This is a very highly regarded site, one of the first, and still one of the best. Students will also enjoy the fun and games section.

Dinsoauria

http://www.dinosauria.com

This site features an excellent gallery of dinosaur images. The text is more suited for high school students, but elementary school students will love the pictures.

Education 4 Kids

http://www.edu4kids.com

Features online flash cards, a math square game, and drills for math tables, time, and money. But there's more than math here. The site also features drills on social studies, language, and the table of elements. Fast loading for questions and answers enhances this site.

Enchanted Learning

http://www.enchantedlearning.com/

This is a commercial site that has excellent resources for young students. Their Great Kids Pages includes information on diverse topics like Antarctica, the French Dictionary, and the Great Wall of China. There are also nursery rhymes, preschool activities, and much more.

Exploratorium

http://www.exploratorium.com

This may be one of the best websites period, educational or not. The online exhibits range from building scale models of the solar system to trying to hit a fastball, and all are educational. There's nothing else to say except you really should visit this site.

Fun School

http://www.funschool.com

Funschool offers free online games that are of some educational value, too. The games are divided by grade level, from preschool to 6th.

Funbrain

http://www.funbrain.com/kidscenter.html

Touching on mathematics, language arts, geography and culture, Funbrain presents free learning games for all ages. Additionally, they offer curriculum guides for teachers to use along with the games.

4kids Treehouse

http://www.4kids.com

This is an excellent site that features links to other popular places on the Web in the following categories: reading, science, social studies, entertainment, playroom, and projects. The reading and social studies sections are standouts.

Global Show-n-Tell Home Page

http://www.telenaut.com/gst

Literacy isn't just reading and writing. Artwork, too, is a method of displaying your knowledge and appreciating the insights of others. This page lets children show their work to kids around the world and includes many links to children's art works on the Web.

Homework Central

http://www.homeworkcentral.com

Divided into three sections (grades 1–6, middle & high school, college & beyond) this site is a categorical list (like Yahoo!) of websites. Designed to help students find more information about their homework subject—not to do their homework for them.

Homework Doctor

http://www.sermonillustrator.org/homeworkdoctor/

A good site that contains a categorical list of links to many academic disciplines. Offers a very useful foreign language translation service. The site is geared mainly toward middle school grades.

How Stuff Works

http://www.howstuffworks.com

Many articles on how different things work, including articles on: engines and motors, electronics, household items, basic technologies and computers and the Internet.

How Things Work

http://howthingswork.virginia.edu/

From the author of a physics book on how everyday things works, this site features questions and answers about (obviously) how things work.

Journey North

http://www.learner.org/jnorth/

Take your students on a journey as they study wildlife migration. The program begins each spring and fall and includes a full year of activities to stimulate student inquiry and enthusiasm. This is a very good site.

Kidlink

http://www.kidlink.org/english/general

Kidlink promotes the global dialogue by facilitating contact between kids up to the age of 15. Whole classes or individuals can join after answering four questions. They are then put in contact with other participants who hail from more than 150 different countries.

KidPub (WWW Publishing)

http://kidpub.org/kidpub/

Another place for kids to publish their stories on the Web. Very cool site. Students can also read stories from other kids, add a paragraph to an unfinished story, and even publish their work as a classroom project.

Kids Com

http://www.kidscom.com/

This is a great place for kids to explore the Internet and interact with electronic pals. Games and arts and crafts are provided. Users must register (free) to view the entire site. There is a section for teachers, too. Be aware that this is a commercial site and they do seem most interested in selling things.

Kids Space

http://www.kids-space.org

Another site featuring kids' artwork, this one features the art of children done in English and Japanese. Students can also share stories and musical works. This non-profit organization also offers a penpal service, a bulletin board, and a place for students to post their homepages.

Learn2.com

http://www.learn2.com

A highly-awarded site that features online lessons in hundreds of topics, from cleaning a stereo to learning French and Spanish. Categories: Food and Drink, Healthier Living, Hobbies, Communication, Finance, Childcare, Cleaning, Computers, Automotive, and more.

Legend of Captain Dave's Lost Treasure

http://www.dcls.org/pirate/

If you would like to do a unit on pirates, bring your class to this website. It's set up as an Internet treasure hunt. Students gather answers to the questions by reading the text , deciphering the clues, and submitting their answer. It's a very entertaining and educational hunt.

Mathematics with Alice

http://library.advanced.org/10977

A trip through Algebra with Alice in Wonderland. Good site to direct students to. Especially notable is the problematic board.

National Geographic Society Xpeditions

http://www.nationalgeographic.com/xpeditions/

This site provides resources and learning experiences that conform to the national geographic standards. Users can interact with the exhibits and each other. The site also provides excellent links to a map collection and to related sites on the Web.

National Wildlife Federation KidZone

http://www.nwf.org/kids/

This site features four different games and tours of water, wetlands, endangered species, and public lands. Kids can explore the outdoors through activity lessons posted on the site.

PBS Kids

http://pbskids.org/

Yet another PBS site, this one is dedicated to giving kids a safe place on the Internet. Kids can choose their favorite PBS show and find related activities, or click the coloring pages, music, games, stories, or talent show links.

Think Quest

http://www.thinkquest.org

Think Quest, a non-profit organization, sponsors contests that challenge learners of all ages to create high-quality, innovative, and content-rich websites. Prizes include over a million dollars in scholarships and awards. Be sure to check out their Library of Entries.

TIME for Kids

http://www.timeforkids.com

The popular weekly news magazine has a special edition online for kids. Includes a multimedia section that usually focuses on science and technology. Probably best for middle and high school students.

Virtual Field Trips

http://www.field-guides.com

Excellent site. Take your students on a field trip without ever leaving the classroom, doing a headcount or wondering where little Johnny ran off to. Trips now available include fierce creatures, tornadoes, deserts, hurricanes, the natural wonders of the world, salt marshes and volcanoes.

Wacky Web Tales

http://www.hmco.com/hmco/school/tales

This site is a great grammar teacher. Students fill out an online form and, based upon their word choices, create Wacky Web Tales. Geared more towards upper elementary students (4th grade and up). It is kind of like the old Mad Libs books.

Why Files

http://www.rpi.edu/~sofkam/isuny/why-files.html

A long list of questions (and answers) to life's little mysteries. A good place for kids to visit to learn something they have always wondered about and to get story ideas that are different and fun.

Yahooligans! The Web Guide for Kids

http://www.yahooligans.com

This is a Yahoo! search engine for kids featuring the sites they may be most interested in. There are many links to websites as well as sections on games, jokes, reference resources, and sports. This is a good site for the students to begin their web searching.

Software

Software

To take full advantage of the Internet, you'll need software. The good news is that most of the software is free. The sites listed below are software download sites with explanations about each program. Please note that each software program has certain system requirements, so read the notes before deciding whether or not the software will work on your computer. If you fail to do so, these programs may cause problems.

Browsers

To view web pages, you are going to need a browser. The most popular browser (with over 90% market share) is Microsoft's Internet Explorer. Other popular browsers include Netscape and Opera. Browsers read the HTML code (Hypertext Markup Language) and render the pages for viewing. They can also do a lot more, depending on which version you download. Both Internet Explorer and Netscape Navigator come with other free software, including a web page editor, a newsgroup viewer and an e-mail program. The downloads are available in different configurations (browser only, browser and e-mail program, etc.). Make sure your computer system meets the minimum requirements suggested by the software maker. These are usually long downloads over a dial-up modem, so be prepared to wait awhile. Go to the "downloads" or "products" section of the sites listed below for more information.

Microsoft Internet Explorer
http://www.microsoft.com

Netscape Navigator
www.netscape.com

Opera
http://www.opera.com/

Other Browsers
http://www.browsers.com

Chat

Chat is often confused with the Web, since many websites offer a chat application as part of their site. Real chatters, though, know that chat is much more than just a feature on a website. One very popular chat application is Internet Relay Chat (IRC). IRC allows you to set up a chat room, or join any of the thousands already established. You'll find one (or many) IRC rooms on just about any topic you can think of. Another popular chat application is Microsoft's NetMeeting. NetMeeting allows you to talk and see the people you are chatting with (requires microphone and a web cam). You can also share documents and programs and use a whiteboard simultaneously. Go to the "downloads" or "products" section of the sites listed below for more information.

mIRC

http://www.mirc.com/

Netmeeting

http://www.microsoft.com

E-mail Service

Many sites now offer free e-mail service. The sites vary by services offered. Some allow just for text e-mail, while others allow for attachments, pictures, and more. Many people obtain one of these free e-mail addresses for the following practical reason: On some sites, it is required that you give your e-mail address before downloading a program or accessing some special part of the site. After you have given them the address, you may start receiving Spam (unsolicited advertisements) in your inbox. If you obtain a free e-mail address from one of these services, you can give that e-mail address out and keep the Spam from coming into the e-mail you use for work and personal reasons. Here are some of the more popular free e-mail services:

Yahoo

http://www.yahoo.com

Excite

http://www.excite.com

Hotmail

http://www.hotmail.com

E-mail Software

Believe it or not, e-mail software programs are also available for free. You'll find that these programs offer many of the same features found on pay-e-mail programs, including filtering, support for multiple e-mail addresses, and other features. Some e-mail programs, like Microsoft's Outlook Express, come as part of the browser package while others, like Eudora Lite, are available as stand-alone downloads. Go to the "downloads" or "products" section of the sites listed below for more information.

Outlook Express

http://www.microsoft.com

Netscape

http://www.netscape.com

Eudora Lite

http://www.qualcomm.com

Newsgroups (USENET)

One of the most overlooked parts of the Internet is the USENET. The USENET is text-based communications forum, divided into over 60,000 newsgroups, each one devoted to a specific topic. Everyday, millions of messages are posted to the USENET. Users may also post images and files, though the USENET is not the best vehicle to transfer files since the USENET servers impose a size limitation on the messages. Instead, the USENET is used more for community building through text messages. People with similar interests post and read messages and become virtual friends without ever having met. The USENET is accessed through a newsreader program. Most new browsers include a free newsreader program as part of the browser, though there are very good newsreader applications available elsewhere.

Instant Messaging Software

Instant Messaging software allows you to send instant messages, of course. This is thought desirable over e-mail because: 1) your messages arrive instantly on the computer of the person you sent the message to, and 2) you can do more than send messages, like send files and open up chat rooms. After you first install an Instant Messenger software program, you add your friends and colleagues (who are also using that same Instant Messenger) to your list. You will then be able to see who is online and available to receive Instant Messages. There are provisions in some of these software programs for you to remain "invisible," that is, you are running the Instant Messenger software but you appear to be off-line to other users. Of course, if you are online and not running the software, you are unavailable to them anyway, but some people like to run the software and appear off-line to the others just so they can monitor who is actually online (it's kind of like screening your calls).

Instant Messaging software is very popular. ICQ has over 35 million users and AOL claims a similar number (although some users have probably registered multiple times). The one drawback to these programs is that they cannot communicate with each other, so if you are using ICQ and your friend has AOL Instant Messenger, you cannot share messages (even though AOL owns ICQ! Figure that one out). Microsoft and Yahoo! have built into their messenger programs the ability to communicate with AOL Instant Messenger users, but AOL keeps changing their software to keep this feature from working. Most industry experts have sided with Microsoft and Yahoo! and called for open standards, so the day may soon come when one program will be able to communicate with the other. We'll see.

Instant Messenger Software

AOL Instant Messenger
http://www.aol.com

Like ICQ and MSN Instant Messenger, AOL's Instant Messenger allows you to send instant messages to other AOL Instant Messenger users. With so many choices of Instant Messaging software, you may want to make your decision based on what your friends and colleagues use. For the most part (except for MSN Messenger) one instant messaging software cannot talk to any of the others.

ICQ
http://www.icq.com (Windows, Mac)

ICQ (read out loud: "I Seek You") is an instant messaging program. It monitors which of your friends are online and running the ICQ program. When a friend is online, you can send a message that instantly (more or less) appears on their computer. Faster than e-mail, ICQ also allows you to share files, send urls, and even send voice messages.

MSN Messenger (Windows, Mac)
http://messenger.msn.com/

The MSN Messenger is like ICQ. You can send instant messages to other MSN Messenger users. New features are being added all the time. You can now share files, talk on the phone, and share your computer.

Yahoo! Messenger (Windows, Mac)
http://messenger.yahoo.com/

The Yahoo! Messenger offers many of the same features as the others, including buddy lists. Yahoo! also features voice chat, a Yahoo! Search bar, and an interface with Yahoo! Mail.

Special Education

Asperger's Disorder/Autism

Asperger's Disorder Home Page
http://www.aspergers.com/

Asperger's Syndrome
http://www.wpi.edu/~trek/aspergers.html

Asperger's Syndrome Support Network
http://home.vicnet.net.au/~asperger/

Autism Frequently Asked Questions
http://www.teleport.com/~kjim/autism.shtml

Autism Society of America
http://www.autism-society.org

Center for the Study of Autism
http://www.autism.org

Online Asperger's Syndrome Information and Support
http://www.udel.edu/bkirby/asperger

Society for the Autistically Handicapped
http://www.autismuk.com/

Assistive Technology

Alliance for Technology Access
http://www.ataccess.org/

Assistive Technology Online
http://www.asel.udel.edu/at-online/welcome.html

Center for Applied Special Technology
http://www.cast.org

Equal Access to Software and Information
http://www.rit.edu/~easi

Virtual Assistive Technology Center
http://www.at-center.com

Attention Deficit Disorder

50 Tips on Classroom Management for ADD
http://www.enteract.com/~peregrin/add/50clas.html

ADDitude
http://www.additudemag.com

ADHD News
http://www.adhdnews.com

ADHD Special Needs Resources
http://adhd.kids.tripod.com

Attention Deficit Disorder Frequently Asked Questions
http://www3.sympatico.ca/frankk/addfaq3.txt

Attention Deficit Disorders, Hyperactivity & Associated Disorders
http://www.execpc.com/~calliope

National Attention Deficit Disorder Association
http://www.add.org

One ADD Place
http://www.oneaddplace.com

Teaching Students with ADD/ADHD Resource Guide for Teachers
http://www.bced.gov.bc.ca/specialed/adhd/toc.htm

Down Syndrome

Down Syndrome
http://tqjunior.thinkquest.org/3880/

National Association for Down Syndrome
http://www.nads.org

National Down Syndrome Society
http://www.ndss.org

National Down Syndrome Education and Research Institute
http://web.idirect.com/~ndseri

Down Syndrome *(cont.)*

Up With Downs
http://www.upwithdowns.com/

Dyslexia

Adult Dyslexia Organisation
http://www.futurenet.co.uk/chanty/ado

Dyslexia Center
http://www.dyslexiacenter.com

Dyslexia Institute
http://www.dyslexia-inst.org.uk

Dyslexia—The Gift
http://www.dyslexia.com

International Dyslexia Association
http://www.interdys.org

Recording for the Blind and Dyslexic
http://www.rfbd.org

General

Access Able
http://www.access-able.com

Barriers Compliance
http://www.access-board.gov

Disabilites.org
http://www.disabilities.org

Disability Products
http://www.disabilityproducts.com

New Mobility Magazine
http://www.newmobility.com

Reach Out Magazine
http://www.reachoutmag.com

General *(cont.)*

Stuttering Center
http://www.stuttering.com

Winners on Wheels
http://www.wowusa.com

Disability Organizations

Ability Support Net
http://www.ablelink.com

Accreditation Council
http://www.accredcouncil.org

ADA InfoNet
http://www.ada-infonet.org

Advocacy & Resource
http://www.arc-resources.org

Alliance for Tech Access
http://www.ataccess.org

Arc
http://thearc.org/welcome.html

ASKERIC Home Page
http://ericir.syr.edu

Classroom Management Special Education
http://www.pacificnet.net/~mandel/SpecialEducation.html

Council for Disability Rights
http://www.disabilityrights.org

Council for Exceptional Children
http://www.cec.sped.org

Dana Foundation
http://www.dana.org

Disability Organizations *(cont.)*

Disability Related Sites on the WWW
http://thearc.org/related-links.htm

Family Village - A Global Community of Disability-Related Resources
http://www.familyvillage.wisc.edu/

Internet Resources for Special Children (IRSC)
http://www.irsc.org

Intervention Techniques
http://curry.edschool.virginia.edu/go/cise/ose/information/interventions.html

National Center to Improve Practice in Special Education
Through Technology, Media, and Materials (NCIP)
http://www2.edc.org/NCIP

National Clearinghouse of Rehabilitation Training Materials
http://www.nchrtm.okstate.edu

National Information Center for Children and Youth with Disabilities
http://www.nichcy.org

National Sports Center for the Disabled
http://www.nscd.org

Special Education Resource on the Internet (SERI)
http://seriweb.com/

SNOW (Special Needs Opportunity Windows)
http://snow.utoronto.ca/

Special Olympics
http://www.specialolympics.org

Gifted and Talented

Hoagies' Gifted Education Page
http://hoagiesgifted.org/

Gifted Children
http://www.gifted-children.com

Gifted Education - A Resource Guide for Teachers
http://www.bced.gov.bc.ca/specialed/gifted/toc.htm

Gifted and Talented *(cont.)*

Gifted Resources
http://www.eskimo.com/~user/kids.html

This site provides links to other gifted sites as well as information on talent searches, distance learning programs, scholarships, publications, organizations, mailing lists, etc.

National Association for Gifted Children
http://www.nagc.org

National Foundation for Gifted and Creative Children
http://www.nfgcc.org

National Research Center for Gifted Education & Talent Development
http://www.ucc.uconn.edu/~wwwgt

Hearing Impairment

Alexander Graham Bell Association for the Deaf
http://www.agbell.org

American Sign Language Browser
http://commtechlab.msu.edu/sites/aslweb

Basic Guide to ASL
http://www.masterstech-home.com/ASLDict.html

Council on Education of the Deaf
http://www.deafed.net/

Deaf Resource Library
http://www.deaflibrary.org

Gallaudet University
http://www.gallaudet.edu

Hard of Hearing and Deaf Students Resource Guide for Teachers
http://www.bced.gov.bc.ca/specialed/hearimpair/toc.htm

Learn Sign
http://www.learnsign.com.au/

ADA Documents
http://janweb.icdi.wvu.edu/kinder/document.htm

Laws, Standards, and IEPs

Appendix A—Notice of Interpretation
http://www.edlaw.net

IDEA 97
http://www.ed.gov/offices/OSERS/IDEA

Individualized Education Program: The Process
http://www.ldonline.org/ld_indepth/iep/iep_process.html

Seven Habits of Highly Effective IEP Teams
http://www.ldonline.org/ld_indepth/iep/seven_habits.html

Writing Individualized Education Programs for Success
http://www.ldonline.org/ld_indepth/iep/success_ieps.html

Your Child's IEP—Practical and Legal Guidance for Parents
http://www.ldonline.org/ld_indepth/iep/iep_guidance.html

Learning Disabilities

LD Online
http://www.ldonline.org

LD Resources
http://www.ldresources.com

Learning Disabilities Association of America
http://www.ldanatl.org

Learning Disabilities Center
http://www.coe.uga.edu/ldcenter/resources/adolescents.html

National Center for Learning Disabilities
http://www.ncld.org

Teen Learning Disabilities
http://www.ld.org/livingwithld/teens_home.cfm

Physical Impairment

American Association of People with Disabilities
http://www.aapd.com

Centre for Neuro Skills
http://www.neuroskills.com

Disabled People's International
http://www.dpi.org

National Rehabilitation Information Center
http://www.naric.com

United Cerebral Palsy
http://www.ucpa.org

Visual Impairment
Ability Home Page
http://www.ability.org

American Council of the Blind
http://acb.org

Blindness Resource Center
http://www.nyise.org/blind.htm

National Federation of the Blind
http://www.nfb.org

Recording for the Blind and Dyslexic
http://www.rfbd.org

Teaching

A to Z Teacher Stuff

http://atozteacherstuff.com

More than one million visitors a month visit this site to peruse the many resources for the teacher candidate and the practicing teacher, including teacher tips, thematic units and lesson plans, and suggested book activities.

A World of Kindergartens

http://www.coe.iup.edu/worldofkindergarten/

A very detailed website companion to the Kinder-L mailing list. The site contains curriculum and activity ideas from early childhood teachers. Good site.

American Federation of Teachers

http://www.aft.org

The website from the AFT, featuring current union news, information about boycotts, and AFT press releases.

BiblioCat Webpage

http://members.aol.com/sskufca/

A mega-site of education-related links, all nicely categorized and of interest to librarians, teachers, homeschoolers and parents. You can browse by subject or search the site by keyword.

ProQuest K-12

http://www.proquestk12.com/

ProQuest is the company behind educational technology products like SIRS, eLibrary, and Reading A-Z. ProQuest offers online subscription-based research and educational materials. Visit this site to learn more about their products.

Busy Teacher's K-12 Website

http://www.ceismc.gatech.edu/busyt

This is one of the best meta-sites on the web, featuring hundreds of links to education-related websites. The site has been redesigned to be more easily navigated.

Chalkboard

http://thechalkboard.com

The Chalkboard lists free educational resources offered by corporations, including curricular materials, programs, and services. The site also has information on funding opportunities and job positions.

Creative Teaching

http://www.creativeteachingsite.com/

The Creative Teaching website offers articles, ideas, and information on teaching styles and creative teaching methods. There are also free handouts, humorous pieces, and other free materials.

Early Childhood Educator's Web Corner

http://users.sgi.net/~cokids/

The index to all things Early Childhood. Hundreds of links in seemingly hundreds of categories. Well-maintained and updated frequently.

Games Kids Play

http://www.gameskidsplay.net

Hundreds of ideas to fill that half-hour of physical education. Includes game descriptions, rules and objectives.

Home School Internet Resource Center

http://www.rsts.net/home/home.html

Featuring a huge list of related links, The Home School Resource Center is a good first-stop if you're looking for information on home schooling. You should be warned, though, that the site seems to be evolving into a more commercial vehicle.

Idea Box - Early Childhood Education and Activity Resources

http://www.theideabox.com

Another site whose title basically describes the content. Also offers a "site of the week," message board on many different topics, and a free monthly newsletter.

iloveteaching.com

http://www.iloveteaching.com/

Full of practical advice and good tips, iloveteaching.com is a good stop for the new teacher. Among the many articles are pieces on student teaching, how to write lesson plans, mentoring, and methods of observation.

Learner.org

http://www.learner.org/

A result of the collaboration between The Annenberg Foundation and the Corporation for Public Broadcasting, Learner.org helps teachers increase their expertise and improve their teaching methods. The Teacher's Lab section, http://www.learner.org/teacherslab/, is the standout of this site as it offers modules on the science of light, space and shape geometry, patterns in math, and the private universe.

Middle School Partnership

http://www.middleschool.com/

If you're a middle school teacher or administrator, this site can help you stay abreast of the latest developments and trends affecting middle schools. At this site, you'll find staff development resources, articles for teachers and administrators, and the latest school news.

MiddleWeb

http://www.middleweb.com

MiddleWeb explores "the challenges of middle school reform." Contains many resources for teachers, including lesson plans in many areas.

National Education Association (NEA)

http://www.nea.org

The union of 2.3 million teachers has put together a very extensive website that contains union news, education and teacher briefs, and even some humor in the Recess section.

New York Times Learning Network

http://www.nytimes.com/learning

Tons of resources for teachers. Daily and archived lesson plans, education news, kid-safe news items, and much more. Geared more for high school students.

Online Schoolyard

http://www.onlineschoolyard.com

This is another meta-site consisting of links to other websites. The Online Schoolyard has good organization and makes finding sites relatively easy.

PBS Online

http://www.pbs.org

The home page for PBS. Offers many educational resources, as well as information about PBS programs.

PBS TeacherSource

http://www.pbs.org/teachersource

Public Broadcasting's website for teachers. Information on PBS educational resources, copyright information, informative articles and more. Very good site.

Preschool By Stormie

http://www.preschoolbystormie.com/

This is a nice site that makes it easy to access its useful resources. There are many tips for the preschool teacher on all facets of teaching. Teachers will also find monthly curriculums, activities, a children's gallery, and more.

Preschool Education

http://www.preschooleducation.com/

Offers many resources for preschool teachers, including bulletin boards, activities, lesson plans, a discussion forum, and much more. The site does suffer, however, from irritating pop-up and embedded advertisements.

Students Can Learn On Their Own

http://users.erols.com/interlac/

This site provides information and resources for the independent student, including a large list of published methods and materials.

CALIN: Cross-Age Learning International Network

http://www.crossagelearning.net/

This is the place to go to learn about cross-age learning, in which older and younger students help each other to grow academically and socially. Here you will find the benefits and justifications of cross-age learning, as well as methods and lesson plans for implementing it in your school.

Teacher Magazine

http://www.teachermagazine.org/

Teacher Magazine is a slick, very informative online magazine. They offer full-length articles reprinted from the print edition.

Teacher's Center

http://www.eduplace.com/teacher

From Houghton Mifflin, this site offers collaborative project ideas, discussion forums, and information on math, language arts, and social studies.

Teacher's Desk

http://www.teachersdesk.org/

The Teacher's Desk contains more than 150 lesson ideas for 5th and 6th grades in spelling, English, writing, and reading. Each lesson idea is fully explained and ready to use. The site also offers block activities, a paragraph a week writing lesson, and more.

Teachers First

http://www.teachersfirst.com

Teachers First offers information to use in the classroom and to use in your professional development. There are many links to pertinent websites and many lesson plans neatly categorized.

Teachers Helping Teachers

http://www.pacificnet.net/~mandel

A private site that offers teachers the opportunity to exchange tips about instruction, classroom management, and anything else that goes on in the classroom. More than just lesson plans!

The Lighthouse for Education

http://www.thelighthouseforeducation.co.uk/home.htm

Although this website serves a school district in England, you will find useful features such as the education web links organized by subject area, the teacher information pages including the best practices links, and the search engine.

Teaching & Learning on the WWW

http://www.mcli.dist.maricopa.edu/tl

A searchable archive of more than 800 examples of how the World Wide Web is being used as a medium for learning. You can search by subject area and see how other teachers are using the web to help their students learn.

Teachnet.com

http://www.teachnet.com

This site features current news on teaching, discussion forums, lesson plans, and many other informative articles about teaching and education.

Tried and True: Tested Ideas for Teaching and Learning

http://www.ed.gov/pubs/triedandtrue

This online book is a rich resource for teachers. Presented by the Regional Educational Laboratories, it covers instructional content and practice, teacher professional development, and school improvement strategies.

What to Expect Your First Year of Teaching

http://www.ed.gov/pubs/FirstYear

This informative booklet from the U.S. Department of Education helps prepare new teachers by offering suggestions on preparation, additional resources, and more.

World Wide Web Virtual Library- Education

http://www.csu.edu.au/education/library.html

This virtual library attempts to catalogue education sites on the Web. There are hundreds of links to education websites arranged in several different ways.

Technology

---

actden Digital Education Network

http://www.actden.com

This site provides free software tutorials on such popular software programs as FrontPage 2000, Office 2000, Internet Explorer, and more. The actden site also offers online courses, a primer on Information Technology, and a lot more.

Apple Education

http://education.apple.com

Apple's education website features tons of useful information for students, teachers, and parents. A little heavy on the Apple propaganda, but still a good site. You'll need a QuickTime and Acrobat viewer for some of these pages (see the multimedia section of this book).

AT&T Learning Network Resources for Educators

http://www.att.com/learningnetwork/teachers/

AT&T offers an online mentoring program that helps teachers to use technology efficiently. They also offer a nice set of categorized links to other education sites as well as other tools useful to teachers.

Cable in the Classroom

http://www.ciconline.com

Cable in the Classroom is a $420 million public service effort supported by 38 national cable networks and over 8,500 local cable companies. Information is provided on various television shows on cable that could be integrated into the classroom. There are also links to participating channels' sites for educators.

Computers, Teachers, Peers

http://www.clp.berkeley.edu/CLP.html

This is a description of a University at California, Berkley, research project where a wired classroom is used by eighth-graders as they are taught the physical science topics of heat, light, and sound.

Electronic School

http://www.electronic-school.com/

This educational technology magazine was published from 1987 to 2002, and is now archived online. You can view entire issues just by clicking your mouse. Try searching the archives to find specific information.

Cybertimes (from the New York Times)

http://www.nytimes.com/pages/technology

The technology section of the New York Times. Contains late-breaking news on technology and its impact on culture, education, etc. Site requires free registration.

David Levin's Learning@Web.Sites

http://www.ecnet.net/users/gdlevin/home.html

This guide is for those high school teachers who wish to enhance their instruction with Internet resources. There are 19 different departments, each with valuable resources for teachers.

Educational Technology Network

http://www.edutechnet.com

Featuring software reviews, best practices information, and informative articles, this site offers a little bit of everything to the teacher interested in exploring the educational technology field.

Electronic Collaboration

http://www.alliance.brown.edu/topics/technology.shtml#item1a

The National School Network has put together (and put online) this guide, Electronic Collaboration: A Practical Guide for Educators. The guide discusses collaboration concepts, how to design and implement a collaborative environment, and what software tools you'll need.

Electronic Elementary Magazine: "The E-LINK"

http://www.inform.umd.edu/UMS+State/MDK12_Stuff/homepers/emag/

This magazine is a nonprofit, educational project that highlights interactive projects and creations of elementary grade students around the world. While it looks as if the site is no longer being updated, the content on the site is worth a look.

Electronic School

http://www.electronic-school.com

Published quarterly as a print and online supplement to The American School Board Journal, this is an excellent magazine site that provides full text articles and information for and about the wired school.

Encyclopedia of Educational Technology

http://coe.sdsu.edu/eet/

Designed primarily for preservice and new teachers, this site uses video to help describe key components of educational technology. There are hundreds of short articles on topics such as cognition, distance education, instructional strategies, and software.

eSchool News online

http://www.eschoolnews.com

A weekly online magazine detailing the latest news in technology/education. A companion site that advertises their print publication, but still worthwhile.

From Now On-The Educational Technology Journal

http://fromnowon.org

Free online journal devoted to educational technology issues. Even though the design is somewhat bare, this journal offers lengthy and informative articles that make the site a regular must-visit for educators interested in technology.

Global Schoolhouse

http://www.gsh.org

Presented by the Global SchoolNet Foundation, this site features The Connected Educator, The Connected Classroom, and The Connected Learning Community.

Harnessing the Power of the Web: A Tutorial

http://www.gsn.org/Web/

An unbelievably detailed lesson on how to integrate the Internet into the classroom. Intended more for secondary education, this tutorial provides step-by-step instructions (and lessons) to using the Web for education.

Intel in Education

http://www.intel.com/education

From the chipmaker Intel, this site offers resources for teachers wishing to integrate technology into their classroom. There are also lessons on how a computer works as well as how various parts of the computer are made. Information on Intel's grants, donations, and scholarships is also available.

Internet Public Library

http://ipl.sils.umich.edu

This site features online lessons covering the Internet and other areas and contains a wide array of resources for students and teachers.

Netiquette Home Page

http://www.albion.com/netiquette/

Netiquette is the online version of etiquette. This site explains the dos and don'ts of the online world. FOR EXAMPLE, WHY YOU SHOULDN'T USE ALL CAPS, avoiding flame wars, and more.

On the Horizon

http://horizon.unc.edu

This site provides a meeting place for educators interested in technology issues. Also available are articles about educational technology research.

Reinventing Schools

http://stills.nap.edu/readingroom/books/techgap/

From the National Academies of Science and Engineering, a companion website to the historic convocation that sought to inform the technology/education debate by "laying out a vision of what could be."

Road Map

http://www.webreference.com/roadmap/

Roadmap96 is a free, 27-lesson Internet training workshop designed to teach new Net travelers how to travel around the rapidly expanding (and often confusing) "Information Superhighway" without getting lost. Very informative!

SuperKids Educational Software Review

http://www.superkids.com

SuperKids offers very detailed educational software reviews. The software is rated based on ease of install, educational value, and kid appeal. Very useful.

SupportNet Online

http://supportnet.merit.edu/

SupportNet Online offers free online courses for teachers interesting in learning more about the networks and operating systems commonly found in schools. The site also contains information on how to create a web club.

Teaching and Learning on the Web

http://www.mcli.dist.maricopa.edu/tl/

The purpose of this site is to show how the Internet is being used as a medium for learning. Use the search engine to find a website that demonstrates online education in a specific subject area.

TeachNet.org

http://www.teachnet.org

TeachNet.org offers teacher-designed projects and activities that incorporate technology. They also offer information on grants and resources for teachers.

tech.Learning

http://www.techlearning.com

The online version of the magazine presents hundreds of software and websites reviews. The Web Tours section is particularly useful, as in the teacher-selected list of websites. Also includes articles on how to integrate technology into the curriculum.

Technological Horizons in Education (T.H.E.)

http://www.thejournal.com

One of the better educational technology publications, T.H.E. offers news on the world of computers and related technologies, focusing on applications that improve teaching and learning for all ages.

Technology Integrations

http://www.mcrel.org/resources/technology/

From the Mid-continent Regional Educational Laboratory, this site offers articles on Internet safety, the impact of technology, funding, school discounts, and technology and teacher education.

Think Quest

http://www.thinkquest.org

Think Quest, a non-profit organization, sponsors contests that challenge learners of all ages to create high-quality, innovative, and content-rich websites. Prizes include over a million dollars in scholarships and awards.

U.S. Kids Compute

http://www.uskidscompute.com

Presented by the Learning Company, U.S. Kids Compute is a program to donate Dr. Seuss-type multimedia to more than 200 communities. This site offers practical tips on computers, a kids and computer FAQ, and more.

Web 66-A K-12 World Wide Web Project

http://Web66.coled.umn.edu

This highly-awarded site has 3 main goals: 1. To help K–12 educators learn how to set up their own Internet servers. 2. To link K–12 Web servers and the educators and students at those schools. 3. To help K–12 educators find and use K–12 appropriate resources on the Web. A very nice site!

Web Developers Virtual Library

http://www.wdvl.com/

This is an indispensable site when you are trying to get that first home page up and running and an even better resource once you get hooked on HTML and want to start doing the fancy things.

Web Page Design for Educators

http://www.uwstout.edu/soe/profdev/teachnet/four/index.html

On this site you will learn everything from the basics of well-designed web pages to how to publicize your completed web page. Explore this site further for more information on how to use the Internet in your classroom.

WebQuest

http://webquest.sdsu.edu/

A WebQuest is an inquiry-oriented activity in which most or all of the information used by learners is drawn from the Web. There is a lot of information available here that will help you create your own WebQuest for your students.

webTeacher

http://www.webteacher.org/winexp/indextc.html

Interested in putting up your own home page but have no idea how to get started? This site will be a great help. It offers a good introductory tutorial to the web for new webmasters.

World Wide Web Workbook

http://sln.fi.edu/primer/primer.html

This is a primer for a person new to the Web. It is appropriate for teachers and students and does an excellent job of covering the basics without talking down to you.

Writing HTML

http://www.mcli.dist.maricopa.edu/tut

Learn to write your own home page by following this tutorial. The lessons are also available offline. It is written in a way so that anyone can understand the subtleties of HTML and designed to take teachers step-by-step through the process of creating Web pages.

www4teachers

http://www.4teachers.org

This website offers a collection of online resources for teachers compiled by teachers. The categories are Professional Development, Stars (examples of technology usage by teachers and students), Integrating Technology, and Tools.

Test Practice

4tests.com

http://www.4tests.com

If your students are curious about the SAT, ACT, or AP tests in Biology, Chemistry, or US History, have them visit this site. 4tests offers sample practice exams on these topics as well as many others (including many computer-related tests). Just beware the many ads and registration process.

Easy Test Maker

http://www.easytestmaker.com/

Easy Test Maker is just what its name implies, a website that allows you to easily make tests that you print for use in the classroom. This site is totally free and one of the best. You can prepare true and false, multiple choice, short answer, matching, and fill-in-the-blank tests. Tests are easily editable, too.

Eisenhower National Clearinghouse-Assessment

http://www.enc.org/topics/assessment

If you need to brush up on the many issues surrounding assessment, this is a good place to start. The ENC has articles on aligning assessment with learning, alternative assessment, strategies for classroom assessment, and standardized testing.

Free Authoring Tool for Web-based Tests

http://www.merexcorp.com/testauthor/

From Merex Corporation, this online tool lets you easily create a test that you can put online. No knowledge of computer code is required. The tests are limited to multiple choice.

FunBrain.com

http://www.funbrain.com/teachers/

The Teachers section of FunBrain.com features the Quiz Lab. For a yearly fee, you can access thousands of online quizzes, edit them for your uses, and have your students take them online. You can also create your own tests. FunBrain offers quiz and item analysis, student reports, and your own classroom home page where you can include links to your tests.

Hot Potatoes

http://web.uvic.ca/hrd/halfbaked/

This is one of the best-known test making programs. It's free for educational use. After installing the program, you will be able to create a variety of tests and then run them on your own computer (PC or MAC). It is not as limited as most online test-making tools but it does require a slightly higher level of technical skill from the teacher.

How to Study

http://www.how-to-study.com/

Before you give that next test, send your students to this site. They'll read about how they can prepare to study and how to listen better. There are also pages on taking notes in class and keeping track of assignments. Concise and to the point, just like good notes should be.

How to Write Tests

http://www.edu.uleth.ca/courses/ed3604/HTWT.html#mc

Featuring a very thorough examination of, well, examinations, this collection of pages will walk you through the hows, whys, whens, and when nots of writing tests. Dr. Robert Runte gives advice on multiple choice, short answer, essay, true and false, and matching tests. Very good site.

Interactive Tests - EduFind Online Test Centre

http://www.edufind.com/test/index.cfm

Your students can use EduFind to take already-existing online tests to improve
their test-taking skills. As a teacher you can post tests for your students to take as
well as monitor their progress. This is a free service provided that you allow
advertising on the test pages and limit the number of students who use it.

Learning with Technology Profile Tool

http://www.ncrtec.org/capacity/profile/profwww.htm

The NCREL has put together a self-assessment that gauges your current teaching
practices (based on your answers) with a set of indicators for engaged learning and
high-performance. You may be surprised by the results!

Mathline

http://www.pbs.org/teachersource/mathline/overview.shtm

The Assessment section of the Mathline site (from PBS) offers many useful
articles, tools, and tips on assessment in the classroom. Learn how to plan
assessments, the basics of alternative assessment, and even the elements that go in
to asking a good question.

National Council on Teacher Quality

http://www.nctq.org/

While the call for more teacher testing still dominates the landscape, others like the
NCTQ are working to develop alternative certification strategies. Their website
offers information on their efforts as well as news about alternative certification
efforts taking place throughout the U.S. This is a partisan site definitely speaking
for just one point-of-view.

Nation's Report Card

http://nces.ed.gov/nationsreportcard/

The only nationally representative and ongoing gauge of student performance, the Nation's Report Card site from the US Department of Education is a collection of statistics and analysis on standardized tests in reading, mathematics, science, writing, U.S. history, civics, geography, and the arts. See how your class compares to the national averages and read the full reports, the test questions, and student responses (very illuminating).

No Child Left Behind

http://www.nclb.gov/

Much of the focus, for good or bad, of the federal government's No Child Left Behind initiative is aimed at assessment, both of the student and of the teacher and school. This website explains the Department of Education's efforts an encompassed by the Act. It offers fact sheets, lists of Key Dates, a bi-weekly newsletter, and information about Reading First.

Preparing Students to Take Standardized Exams

http://intranet.cps.k12.il.us/Assessments/Preparation/preparation.html

Though written for the Chicago Public Schools, the information here applies to all teachers. The highlights include two lengthy documents detailing how to prepare elementary and high school students to take the standardized exams. There is also information on creating rubrics.

Study Guides and Strategies

http://www.iss.stthomas.edu/studyguides/

Joe Landsberger from the University of St. Thomas has put together one of the best sites on studying and test taking. There are many links to all kinds of studying and testing articles. An added bonus—the site is available in 17 different languages! It's obvious that a lot of thought and effort went into this site and you should definitely visit it!

Test Taking Strategies

http://www.byu.edu/ccc/Learning_Strategies/test/strategy.htm

From BYU, this page details many test taking strategies. It is unique, though, because it uses tests within the page to illustrate the strategies necessary for success.

Test Taking Tips and Strategies

http://www.usoe.k12.ut.us/eval/Parenttesttaking.htm

This is a site you can share with students and parents. It covers the basics of test preparation for students but it also talks to parents, telling them how they can help their child perform better on tests.

Writing Multiple Choice Items

http://www.ed.gov/databases/ERIC_Digests/ed398236.html

This is a short article from the ERIC Digest that covers the basics of constructing multiple choice tests. Other guides to test writing can be found at the same address. Just replace the article number with ed398237.html, ed398238.html, and ed398239.html.

Writing

A+ Research and Writing for High School and College Students
http://www.ipl.org/div/aplus/

This site from The Internet Public Library's TeenSpace has a step-by-step guide for researching and writing a paper. Steps include Getting Started, Discovering and Choosing a Topic, Looking for and Forming a Focus, Gathering Information, Preparing to Write, and Writing the Paper. Tips are included for both library and online research.

Guide to Grammar and Writing
http://webster.commnet.edu/grammar/

Guide to Grammar and Writing is a comprehensive site with a large amount of information ranging from parts of a sentence to overcoming writer's block. There are over 170 quizzes, tips for writing research papers, *PowerPoint* presentations to download, and even quotes from writers about writing. A great site for teachers and students alike!

HerCorner
http://www.hercorner.com/

The catchphrase of this site is "when writing feels like a sixth sense," which you may find indicative of the more personal nature of the information to be found here. Find here resources for the woman writer, whether the writing is fiction, nonfiction, a newsletter, or a personal journal. Topics covered include adding your personality to a business ezine, overcoming doubt, and teaching versus preaching.

HyperHandouts from Texas A&M University
http://uwc.tamu.edu/handouts/

Handouts from this site provide an overview of the writing process, from Invention Techniques to Signs of a Rushed Paper. You can also find additional information on grammar and tips for analyzing an article or story. Not sure how to format that memo? Or are you trying to create a cover letter or resume that will really get you noticed? This site can help.

Scriptorium

http://www.thescriptorium.net/

The Scriptorium is an online magazine (or Webzine) for writers. Included are articles on writing, creative exercises to try, book reviews, printable forms for developing characters and self-editing, and software for both Windows and Macintosh users. Make sure that you check out Scriptorium Scribbles, the online Webzine for young writers, which has articles, resources, a workshop, and more! **http://www.thescriptorium.net/youth.html**

University of Richmond's Writer's Web

http://writing.richmond.edu/writing/wweb.html

At the Writer's Web, you can explore writing topics listed by stages of the writing process. Find information on brainstorming ideas, writing in different topic areas, literary terms, analysis and argument, documentation, and peer editing strategies. You can also look through an A-Z topic index or use the search engine to explore the valuable information that can be found here.

Write4Kids.com

http://www.write4kids.com/

Want to write for kids? Have you had an idea for a children's book for years, but never actually sat down to write it? This is the site that can start you on your path. Find tips for getting started, dos and don'ts, what's in, commonly used children's writing terms, advice from publishers, and free e-books to help you. The library provides free articles on Finding Your Voice, Writing Powerful Endings, Writing About Controversial Subjects, and more.

Writer's Resource Center

http://www.poewar.com/

Find here information on finding time to write, writing poetry, the craft of writing fiction and non-fiction, creativity techniques, technical writing, reviews of books about writing, and more. The "Writer, Edit Thyself" article in particular has an excellent overview of the 10 most common problems encountered by editors.

Notes: